How To Build *Attractive* Personality

Keys To Draw People's Admiration, Confidence, Respect And Support

Moses A. Katamani

How To Build *Attractive* Personality

Keys To Draw People's Admiration, Confidence, Respect And Support

Moses A. Katamani

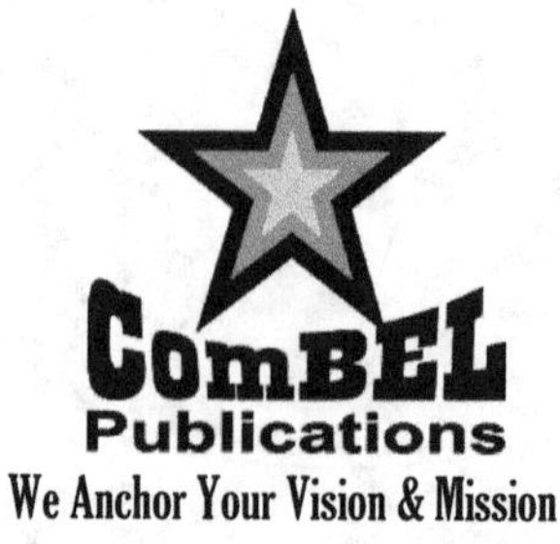

How To Build Attractive Personality

ISBN: 978-9988-1-2605-6

ComBEL Publications
P. O. Box SK 358,
Sakumono-Estates, Tema, Ghana.
Tel: + 233243538726
Email:combelgh@gmail.com
Website: www.combelgh.com*

Cover Design:
EMVICS Graphics
Tel: + 233244654716
E-mail: victoradedje@yahoo.com

Printed By:
ComBEL Print-Press
Email: combelprintpress@gmail.com

Otherwise stated, all scripture quotations are taken from the New King James Versions of the Bible.

CONTENT   PAGE

DEDICATION 

I dedicate this work to the memory of my beloved father; Godfried A. Fudzi. He had been a father who cared very much about his children and has been my source of inspiration and hope.

I also dedicate it to you reader, who believes in developing decent and attractive personality to achieve your Vision and Mission of life. Bravo for the decision to read and own a copy of this book.

*P*utting this work together has been a painstaking one, which required dedicated support behind the scenes, to make it a success. Even though I may not be able to list all my sources of support, I would want to mention a few, who were exceptionally helpful in bringing out this work.

I wish to express my profound gratitude to Jonathan K. Gavi of Brand Ghana office, Akpeko Agbevade, Assistant Registrar: Human Resource and Examinations, University College of Entrepreneurship, Accra, and Juliet Kafui Degadzor for reading through the script and their contributions that have made this work a success. Their scholarly analysis, critics and suggestions have been very valuable.

My heartfelt gratitude goes to my long-time friends Bright Adzroe, District Statistician and Administrator of the Ghana Revenue Authority, Hohoe and Samuel S. Koranteng, a lecturer at the University of Ghana, Legon, Botany Department, for their unflinching support, encouragement, and dedication to my course. I am also very grateful to my compatriots; Wellington, Worla, Mercy and Phyllis for believing in my vision and supporting it.

My gratitude also goes to my book cover designer, Victor Adedje for his patience and tolerance for my constant change of ideas. I also appreciate Wisdom, Jennifer, Kudzo, Francisca and others for their support and diverse assistance. I salute everybody who identifies with my vision and mission.

My deepest thanks go to my mentor and advisers; Rev. S.D.K. Dumevi, Rev. R.M.K. Attih, and Rev. Dr S. K. Ofori for their counsels, prayers, and fiscal support for my visions and projects. Similar thanks go to my pastor, Rev. P.D.K. Tsatsu, and Rev. S.D.K Lodo for their encouragement, spiritual and material supports. In all to God is the glory.

Finally, in spite of the rigorous and meticulous research works done to bring out this piece, there is no doubt that there may be the possibility of an oversight and errors. I singularly take full responsibility for any omission or errors that may be identified.

FOREWORD

*I*t is my pleasure and a privilege to write the forward to this vital theme. I am not too old, but I can remember the wild dreams and ambitions we had prior to my undergraduate days at the University of Ghana, Legon, where I met the author of this book. Names and personalities that were famous at our time were individuals who can boast of their physical strengths and prowess such as the Casanovas and the James Bonds.

Looking back now and reading this book, it says it all that, whilst such memoirs always raises eyebrows; names of attractive personalities are mentioned with dignity and respect, because the heights of these nobles were attained by engaging their neurons. It is certain that as a man thinks in his heart, so is he! If you think you can have an attractive personality, you are on the right course.

This value in your hand is a synopsis of hard to get, scattered and expensive must-haves that is brewed in this crucible "How To Build Attractive Personality". It is not surprising that individuals like you holding this book at this time are different from the masses. It challenges you to think outside the box by harnessing inputs from varied fields of knowledge.

Hearing from Moses A. Katamani at long last is not only timely to encourage the big-shots in society in order to have followers due to their attractive personality and integrity; but as a reference for people who are in search of outstanding personality to brace the challenges of this generation and beyond.

Writing the talk in this book no doubt confirms that there is more up the sleeves of Moses. Having distinguished himself as a seasoned and promising inspirational author and speakers, it is not uncertain that he is taking over from the forerunners.

As a respected tutor who has won the reputation of mothers of his students, he has given priority to your needs. It is not worth moving on without reading the entire piece which is a timely gift for a cherished one like you.

Raymond E.K. Doe
Human Development Expert
University of Science and Technology
Trondhein-Norway

INTRODUCTION

*P*eople would like to follow others, but not just anybody. If you desire to draw people to yourself, you need to develop an appealing personality and character which is admirable and attractive.

I decided to write this book out of years of experience with students, youths and professionals who desire to enhance their personality and become influential, but without much adequate resource book to guide them. Many people fail job interviews not because they are academically incapable or does not have the requisite skills, but due to low self-esteem, whilst some are denied promotion to some positions due to lack of personal appeal. With all these, this work is intended to help readers identify factors which hinder personal attraction, work on them and enhance your personality and self-esteem.

Some people have good ideas, but due to lack of adequate interpersonal and communication skills, are not able to relay their ideas. Some people also have good physical looks, but what comes out of their mouth, will put you off entirely. They cannot keep companies, because of their verbal and nonverbal communication problems. All these are identified and addressed to help enhance your interpersonal and communication skills.

The work is not just imaginative, but out of years of research and experiences. My working experiences for over a decade as a Tutor, Communicator, years of private and voluntary works, especially with the youth have been brought to bear on the work. Though the experiences are not stated directly, they inform my conceptualisation. These have also enlightened me about how our personality affects our daily lives, interpersonal relations and the need to have a resource book which will guide people in pursuing their dreams and becoming outstanding personalities in society.

Many people denigrate others and those who suffer this sort of denigrations accept it and allow it to affect their self-image, self-esteem and personal confidence. Others also think of themselves as people without potentials. But there is no begging the fact that, everybody created in the image of God has some personal strength which makes them unique from other people. There is no doubt that, this book will help you discover or rediscover yourself and boost your personality.

The work is organised into nine chapters. It looks at what is personality and attractive personality. It examines the general classifications of behaviour and the four classifications of temperament. The four temperaments are discussed to help you identify your temperament and the significance of temperament for your personality development. Also discussed are traits society appreciates and steps to build good interpersonal relationships.

It examines personality plus or charisma, looks at some personalities with appealing qualities and how these qualities draw people to them. Again it looks at communication skills and how to improve on your nonverbal skills, how to build personal confidence, trust and what l call "Six L-Rules of Drawing People to Yourself." It concludes with inspirational message which will encourage, motivate and inspire you. In fact this is a book which should be read by students, youths, public speakers, public relations officers, journalists, politicians, civil and public servants, educators, religious and corporate leaders and all people who desire to achieve a fulfilling life.

The work is an integrated study; educative, informative and inspirational. Every subject that is discussed is defined or explained with examples. The examples cut across practical life experiences as noted earlier, wise sayings, research works and biblical illustrations. It is an integrated study which cuts across varied subject areas. This technique is used to help readers understand the concepts and principles in the various subject areas and their effects on our personality.

I hope this work, which is more of 'Personality and Relationship Guide' or better still 'A Road Map to Personal Development," will help you build an attractive and admirable personality to draw the right people to you, to achieve your Vision and Mission for life. "Going up you need people, to excel you need people, everybody need somebody."

Come let's make the journey together for a wonderful expedition. I wish you an amazing and remarkable life experience, as you read this book.

CHAPTER ONE

WHAT IS ATTRACTIVE PERSONALITY?

Many people with good physical look; very handsome or beautiful by all standards, wonder why some people would not want to keep their company. Others could not keep very important relationships and they wonder why. What most of these people could not appreciate is that, their personality or character expels people from them.

People would like to follow others, but not just anybody. If you desire to draw people to yourself, you need to develop an appealing personality and character which is admirable. According to Rick Gettle "In every walk of life, there is a common desire most people have: To be - liked, loved, popular, attractive, admired, respected, recognised, listened to, and considered important. To achieve this goal, a person would have to develop many positive qualities."

> **P**eople would like to identify with or follow others, but not just anybody. If you want to identify with the eagles, you must develop the character of an eagle. Your personality traits can alienate you from people of virtue. To soar higher with the eagles to achieve your vision and mission, you must work on your personality and character to bring out the best qualities in you.

The word 'personality' is derived from the Latin word 'persona' which means 'mask'. It is understood as the study of 'masks' that people wear. It is the inner part of psychological experience which is collectively called your 'self.' Personality actually means the "mask" or inner aspect of a person that is exhibited which goes beyond the outward appearance alone.

According to Carl Gustav Jung (1934), a Psychologist, "Personality is the supreme realisation of the innate idiosyncrasy (peculiarity) of a living being. It is an act of high courage flung in the face of life, the absolute affirmation of all that constitutes the individual, the most successful adaptation to the universal condition of existence coupled with the greatest possible freedom for self-determination."

This definition indicates that the individual has some unique traits, which make you who you are, and these traits go through transformations. They are defining qualities of a person, especially those distinguishing personal characteristics that make you distinct from others. For instance, a person with exceptional intelligence, behaviour or a person with remarkable reputation. The individual has greater amount of freewill to live and portray a type of personality.

A contemporary definition by Carver and Scheier (2000), states that "Personality is a dynamic organisation, inside the person, of psychophysical systems that create a person's characteristic patterns of behaviour, thoughts, and feelings." They further explain the definition as:

- "Dynamic Organisation: it suggests ongoing readjustments, adaptation to experience, continual upgrading and maintaining personality does not just lie there. It has a process and it is organised.
- Inside the Person: suggests internal storage of patterns, supporting the notion that personality influences behaviours.
- Psychophysical systems: suggests that the physical is also involved in 'who we are.'
- Characteristic Patterns: implies consistency or continuity which are uniquely identifying of an individual.
- Behaviour, Thoughts, and Feelings: indicates that personality includes a wide range of psychological experience.
- Manifestation: that personality is displayed in MANY ways."

From these definitions, we can say personality is the sum total of an individual's 'self,' which includes transforming organisation, inner character; behaviour, thoughts, and emotional makeup; *the inside-out of a person*. It is the combination of emotional, intellectual abilities, and moral qualities that distinguish an individual's character, complexion, disposition, and other personal makeup.

A related word used to describe personality is character. Character is defined as "Moral quality; the principles and motives that control life; as, a man of character; his character saves him from suspicion." Or character as "the peculiar quality or the sum of qualities, by which a person is distinguished from others; the stamp impressed by nature, education or habit; that which a person really is; nature; disposition." Perspectives of Character are:

- Unusual person: qualities of your persona.
- Quality of values: morally good qualities.
- Principles of life: intentions that control life.
- Lifestyle or reputation that differentiates a person from others.

With these points of view, character can be described as good personal quality of honesty, politeness, compassion, mental-fortitude and living by the 'progressive rules and regulations' of life which are your guiding principles. You can have positive character or negative character. Positive character traits are good qualities that are appreciated by society; it is a virtuous life. Negative character traits are deviant traits that are detested by society; they are social vices.

Both words; personality and character have similar interpretations, but personality emphasises a person's innate abilities, physical makeup, behaviour, and how they are exhibited, whereas character highlights a person's moral disposition. Personality is the umbrella term used to explain personal characteristics, while character is a sub-set of personality. They describe a person, what drives a person's life and things that differentiate one person from others.

A person's character can either be described as good or bad, right or wrong depending on what the society or societies accept or despise. The value system of the society shapes your personality and character. Other descriptions of a person's personality are:

- The aggregate of features and traits that form the nature of an individual;

- Moral or ethical quality: a man of fine honourable character; qualities of honesty, courage, or the like;
- Integrity, reputation: good repute, an honest secretary;
- An account of qualities or peculiarities of a person;
- A person, especially with reference to behaviour: an admirable or suspicious character.

From all the discussions, an individual's personality can be identified in the following areas: behaviour, psychological makeup, intelligence or cognitive makeup, temperament, emotional disposition, moral or ethical standard, physical looks or appearance and thought patterns.

Factors that Influence Your Personality

There are varied views of the factors that affect personality. Fundamental among them are hereditary and environmental factors. Hereditary factors are genetic features which are inherited or transmitted from parents to their offspring which include intelligence, and physical features like height and complexion. These are innate basic factors which affect the makeup of the individual's personality. Parents' complexion, intelligence or height can be transmitted to their children.

On the other hand, environmental factors are things which influence our daily life from the environment. These among other things are factors which affect personal development such as ethical and social standards of the society. Your social environment such as a village, town, city setting, school, working environment, cultural norms and friends influence your behaviour and personality.

Nonetheless, Bandura Albert (1986), a Clinical Psychologist asserts that, behaviour is not only influenced by internal forces inherited or the environment. He thought that human behaviour occurs as a result of multiple interplay between cognitive and other inner processes, behaviour, and environmental influences, largely based on previous experiences.

The concept states that cognitive and other personal factors, behaviour, and environmental influences operate interactively as determinants of each other. People do not only react to environmental events; they also actively create their own environments or act to change them. Cognitive events determine which environmental events will be perceived and how they will be interpreted, organised and acted upon.

Feedbacks from behaviour, on the other hand, either positive or negative, influence how people think, and the way they act to change the environment. The idea is illustrated in the diagram below.

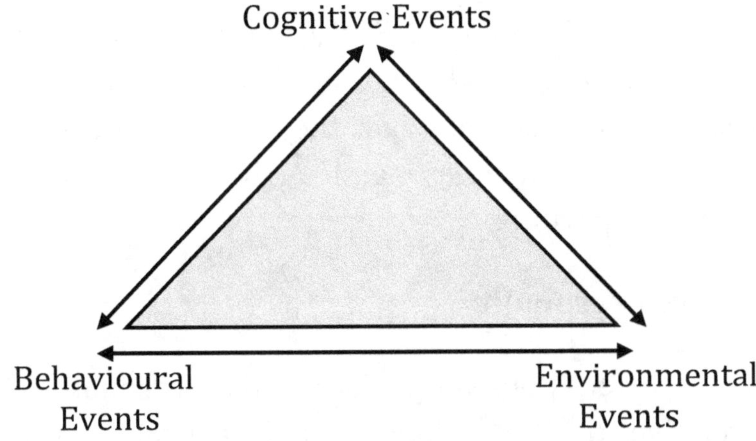

From the diagram, how you think affects your actions and inactions, and influences your environment. Your behaviour affects what you think and also influence your environment. Finally, your environment influences how you think and your behaviour. Therefore, your cognitive events based on the amount of information you have, and other personal factors such as physical features, behavioural events, and environmental events interact to bring out your personality.

In that case, how people relate to you is also based on their cognitive events, depending on the amount of information they have, and other personal factors such as their intelligence level, personal conducts and the environmental influences such as ethical standards or way of life of the society. For example, in the work place, at home or any other social relationships, people appreciate you based on what they know or personal information, behaviour and what the social environment permits.

Attractive Personality

As of the discussions above, attractive personality is the relative positive human traits appreciated by society, which draw the individual to others. They are the positive collective patterns of character, behaviour, temperament, emotional and mental traits, ethical and moral dispositions that draw people to you.

In other words, they are the unique qualities that you have, especially your distinguishing personal characteristics that make you special and socially admirable. Thus, everybody has some personal traits which, when developed, can draw you to others. It is very important for every individual to cultivate a personality that will prove attractive and acceptable to most people. To become admirable, popular and attractive to people you must work on your personal traits to enhance your self-worth.

For your personality to become attractive, you should develop personal qualities such as worthy behaviour, good interpersonal and communication skills which are discussed in the subsequent chapters. Nevertheless, these qualities should not be used as a source of power to intimidate or undermine people.

You should not use your attractive looks, intelligence, eloquence or your social status as a source of power to outdo other people. They should be used genuinely to enhance the life of people. Positive personal traits draw people to you, but self-aggrandisement expel them from you.

CHAPTER TWO

TEMPERAMENT AND YOUR PERSONALITY

*T*he human personality has various characteristics as discussed earlier. One such characteristic which affects your personality and how you relate to people is your temperament. Temperament is the part of your personality which is genetically based. It refers to the innate aspects of an individual's personality.

According to Encyclopaedia Britannica, in psychology, "temperament is the aspect of personality concerned with emotional dispositions and reactions, and their speed and intensity; the term is often used to refer to the prevailing mood or mood pattern of a person."

It refers to how we react to situations and the manner of emotional expressions. There are several works on behaviour and temperament by psychologists. There are general classifications of behaviour, the four classifications of temperament and Tim LaHaye's study from the religious perspective.

General Classification of Behaviour

The general classification of behaviour looks at a person's disposition as extrovert or introvert. "An extrovert is basically a person who is energised by being around other people, while an introvert is a person who is energised by being alone and whose energy is drained by being around other people." This concept was popularised by the work of Carl Gustav Jung.

An extrovert, also known as extravert is mainly concerned with obtaining satisfaction from what is outside the 'self.' They take pleasure in activities that involve large social gatherings, such as get-togethers, neighbourhood or group activities, public protests, and demonstrations.

An extraverted person is likely to enjoy time spent with people and find less reward in time spent alone. They tend to be energised when around other people, they often think best, when they are talking, and they are more prone to boredom when they are by themselves. Concepts just do not seem real to them unless they can talk about them; reflecting on them is not enough.

Introverts on the other hand, tend to be more reserved and less assertive in social situations. They often take pleasure in solitary activities such as reading, writing, drawing, and using computers. An introvert mostly enjoy time spent alone and find less reward in time spent with large groups of people, though they tend to enjoy interactions with close friends. They prefer to concentrate on a single activity at a time and like to observe situations before they take part. Introverts are easily weighed down by too much stimulation from social gatherings and engagements. They often shun social situations, because being around people drain them off their energy. They are more analytical before speaking, and enjoy working alone.

In the view of Hans Eysenck, extroverts seek excitement and social activity in an effort to heighten their arousal level, whereas introverts tend to avoid social situations in an effort to keep such arousal to the minimum. In this vein, an introvert is not simply a person who is shy, but rather less assertive in social situations, while extroverts enjoy social interactions and large social gatherings.

Eysenck compare these traits to the four temperaments, with Choleric and Sanguine temperaments equating to extraversion, and Melancholic and Phlegmatic temperaments equating to introversion.

Keep in mind, however that most people are to some extent of a blend of extrovert and introvert characteristics. In order to improve your behaviour, you need to discover your behaviour pattern, develop the positives and deal with the weaknesses. It helps you relate to people, and manage your social interactions.

The Four Classifications of Temperament

The four temperament theory is an ancient system formulated to help us understand human nature by dividing them according to their basic temperament. Each type is defined by a list of descriptive characteristics. Then people are assigned to one or more types by matching the person with those descriptive characteristics.

The four classification of temperament is based on Claudius Galen's physiological theory of the four basic body fluids (humours): blood, phlegm, black bile, and yellow bile. Depending on the relative prevalence of these fluids in the individual's body, they are supposed to produce, temperaments designated as Sanguine (warm, pleasant), Phlegmatic (slow-moving, apathetic), Choleric (quick to react, hot tempered), and Melancholic (depressed, sad).

Sanguine

Sanguine (warm, pleasant) indicates the personality of an individual with the temperament of blood, night, and the season of spring; wet and hot. A person who is sanguine is generally light-hearted, fun loving, a people person, loves to entertain, spontaneous, optimistic and with leadership qualities. They are mostly friendly people, and they are at ease in social situations.

However, they can be haughty, over-confident, indulgent or take things for granted. They can be day-dreamy and off-task to the point of not accomplishing much and can be reckless, possibly acting on whims in an unpredictable fashion. They act by impulse. They are blind to the effect their actions or decisions may have on other people.

Phlegmatic

Phlegmatic (slow-moving, apathetic) pertains to phlegm, which corresponds to the season of winter; wet and cold, and connotes the element of water. Phlegmatic person is calm and with minimal emotions. They are very consistent, relaxed, rational, curious, and observant, making them good managers and negotiators. Like the sanguine personality, the phlegmatic has many friends.

Whilst phlegmatics are generally self-content and kind, their introverted personality often inhibit enthusiasm in others and make them quite lazy and resistant to change. The lack of passion inherent in the phlegmatic makes them indifferent in relationship with others. They are mostly cynical and procrastinate easily. But the phlegmatic is more reliable and compassionate; these characteristics typically make them more dependable.

Choleric

Choleric (quick to react, hot tempered) corresponds to the fluid of yellow bile, the season of summer; dry and hot, and the element of fire. A person who is choleric is a doer; they are likely to be "great achievers." They have a lot of ambition, energy, and passion, and try to instil it in others. They motivate or inspire people to action.

The choleric champion ideals which are based on recognition of higher goals than some others can understand. They can dominate people of other temperaments, especially phlegmatic types. Many great charismatic political figures are choleric. They are easily angered, ill-tempered and vindictive sometimes. The choleric's strength is zeal, his weakness is anger.

Melancholic

Melancholic (depressed, sad) also known as Melancholy, is associated with the season of autumn; dry and cold, and the element earth. It is the personality of an individual characterised by black bile. A person who is a thoughtful ponderer has a melancholic disposition. A melancholic is also often a perfectionist, being very particular about what they want and how they want it in some cases. They are very intelligent, analytical, creative, and artistic.

These often results in being unsatisfied with one's own artistic or creative works and always pointing out to themselves what could and should be improved. Often very kind and considerate, melancholic can be highly, but also can become overly pre-occupied with tragedy and cruelty around them, thus becoming depressed and moody. Their introverted characteristics make them shy away from or avoid social situations.

Tim LaHaye's Perspective and Temperament Test

Tim illustrates the four temperaments with modern language terms of emotional characteristics and biblical characters which help us identify with the biblical characters in relation to our temperament. Examine the table below.

Table of Equivalents for the 4 Personality Types				
D.E.S.A.	Dominant	Expressive	Solid	Analytical
Hippocrates Greek Terms (370 BC)	Choleric	Sanguine	Phlegmatic	Melancholy
Biblical Characters	Paul	Peter	Abraham	Moses
Disc	Dominance	Influence	Steadiness	Cautious Compliance
Source: Tim LaHaye's illustrations with some modification				

From the table illustrations, Choleric are dominant, the Sanguine are Expressive, with the Phlegmatic being Solid, while the Melancholy are Analytical. The Dominants are doers, Expressive are talkers, Analytical are thinkers, and Solids are much relaxing.

Again, from the table, with biblical inferences Paul is an outgoing person and always on the move to do something, with eagerness, hence Choleric, whereas Peter likes expressing himself on issues and very influential which identify him as Sanguine. Abraham is very steady, reliable, peace maker and faithful to God which classify him as Phlegmatic, whilst Moses is analytical and considerate which identify him as more of Melancholic. You can improve your personality by the behavioural, and temperament studies, if you identify yours.

Tim LaHaye also prescribed two ways of testing to identify your temperament. They are the simple test and the alternative one which is more detailed. Let us use the simple test, then the alternative one.

Simple Test

Read the following questions and answer them to identify your basic temperament.

1. Are you an extrovert or an introvert?
2. Are you a spontaneous quick-talker?
3. Do you have to apologise frequently?
4. Do you have high emotional responses?
5. Are you quiet and slow of speech?
6. Are you a good speller?
7. Do you do well at maths and detail?
8. Do you get depressed easily?

According to Tim LaHaye, if your response to question 1 is extrovert and you answered question 2-4 yes, then your temperament is Sanguine. If you answer yes to only one of 2-4, you are possibly a Choleric. A Melancholy will reply to question 1 as introvert and yes to 6-8. A Phlegmatic will respond yes to question 5 and say 'not easily depressed' to question 8.

Thus, suppose you respond yes you are extrovert to question 1. You agree to question 2 that you are impulsive quick-talker. Apologies frequently and have high emotional responses, then you are Sanguine. Nonetheless, if you reply that you are introvert to question 1, you are a good speller as in question 6, you do well in maths, and easily depressed, then, you are a Melancholic.

The Alternative Test

The alternative test indicates that one person can fall within two or more categorise of temperament. The primary temperament will have the highest score, whilst the secondary temperament follows. The numbers 1-5 refer to the degree of prominence of the characteristics, with 1 being least prominent score and 5 being most prominent score.

In order to have accurate test it is important to set yourself aside to prevent the influence of other people on the outcome. It must be carried out independently for you to have a result which reflects your true nature.

Sanguine   **Scores**

Emotional	1	2	3	4	5
Compassionate	1	2	3	4	5
Impractical	1	2	3	4	5
Easily Discouraged	1	2	3	4	5
Undisciplined	1	2	3	4	5
Difficulty Keeping Resolution	1	2	3	4	5
Weak-willed	1	2	3	4	5
Talkative	1	2	3	4	5
Enjoyable	1	2	3	4	5
Friendly	1	2	3	4	5
Restless	1	2	3	4	5
Difficulty Concentrating	1	2	3	4	5
Lives in Present	1	2	3	4	5
Egotistical	1	2	3	4	5
Impulsive	1	2	3	4	5
Difficulty with Appointments	1	2	3	4	5
Optimistic	1	2	3	4	5
Outgoing	1	2	3	4	5

Phlegmatic	**Scores**				
Very Quiet	1	2	3	4	5
Pessimistic	1	2	3	4	5
Introvert	1	2	3	4	5
Not Aggressive	1	2	3	4	5
Spectator in Life	1	2	3	4	5
Indecisive	1	2	3	4	5
Slow and Lazy	1	2	3	4	5
Easy-going	1	2	3	4	5
Calm and Cool	1	2	3	4	5
Efficient	1	2	3	4	5
Dependable	1	2	3	4	5
Witty-dry Humour	1	2	3	4	5
Teases	1	2	3	4	5
Selfish	1	2	3	4	5
Orderly Habits	1	2	3	4	5
Stingy	1	2	3	4	5
Stubborn	1	2	3	4	5
Work Well Under Pressure	1	2	3	4	5

Choleric   Scores

Optimistic	1 2 3 4 5
Goal-oriented	1 2 3 4 5
Self-centred	1 2 3 4 5
Self-sufficient	1 2 3 4 5
Activist	1 2 3 4 5
Domineering	1 2 3 4 5
Aggressive	1 2 3 4 5
Leadership Ability	1 2 3 4 5
Stick-to-itiveness	1 2 3 4 5
Strong-illed	1 2 3 4 5
Hot-tempered	1 2 3 4 5
Insensitive	1 2 3 4 5
Unsympathetic	1 2 3 4 5
Determined	1 2 3 4 5
Decisive	1 2 3 4 5
Sarcastic	1 2 3 4 5
Practical	1 2 3 4 5
Outgoing	1 2 3 4 5

Melancholic   Scores

	Scores				
Deep Feeling	1	2	3	4	5
Sensitive	1	2	3	4	5
Self-centred	1	2	3	4	5
Easily offended	1	2	3	4	5
Self-sacrificing	1	2	3	4	5
Faithful friend	1	2	3	4	5
Lies Behind the Scenes	1	2	3	4	5
Suspicious	1	2	3	4	5
Introspection	1	2	3	4	5
Perfectionist	1	2	3	4	5
Harbours Resentment	1	2	3	4	5
Creative	1	2	3	4	5
Moody	1	2	3	4	5
Critical	1	2	3	4	5
Indecisive	1	2	3	4	5
Pessimistic	1	2	3	4	5
Idealistic	1	2	3	4	5
Introvert	1	2	3	4	5

(Source: 'Why You Act the Way You Do' By Tim LaHaye.)

To score yourself, circle or mark each number which refers to your degree of score. Sum up the scores for each of the temperaments. The one which has the highest score is your primary temperament, the second highest is your secondary temperament, followed by the rest. For instance if you score Sanguine 56, Phlegmatic 62, Choleric 46, and Melancholy 65, it means your primary temperament is Melancholy, while Phlegmatic is the secondary, followed by Sanguine and Choleric.

You can also score yourself based on 3-5 scores only by ignoring 1 and 2 scores, but this will not be as accurate as using all the scores from 1 to 5 for the test. The four temperament model has 12 mixtures such as Mel-Choler, San-Mel, Phleg-Choler, and so on. The order of temperaments in these pairs is based on which temperament is the "dominant" one in an individual.

A study by Richard G. Arno and Phyllis J. Arno (1984) developed the Fifth temperament known as **Supine**. Until then, there were people who were believed to "fit" into none of the four temperaments. Supine is defined as "lying on the back or with the face turned upward." It is regarded as "serving temperament," because these people feel that their value is to serve others. They share the characteristics of both extroversion and introversion.

Supines are identified by strengths, such as a desire to serve, liking people, and with a gentle spirit. They are described as "slow-paced," but does have some amount of emotional energy. However, they harbour feelings of anger, powerlessness and insignificance.

They are generally open to receiving affection and praises, but have problem initiating. They like and need people; nonetheless, they have fear of rejection. Normally, they expect people to read their mind. They are often frustrated, if they are avoided; they expect people to know they want interaction.

Why the Need to Discover Your Temperament

The study of temperament is met with some hullabaloos of whether it is important to study it or not, especially by some religious groups. Nevertheless, knowing your temperament helps you identify your behavioural and emotional pattern, develop your strengths and deal with your shortcomings.

The book of Hosea 4:6 says "My people are destroyed for lack of knowledge: because thou hast rejected knowledge..." In fact, our knowledge of temperament helps us to avoid many troubles of society and manage our own life. The following are some reasons why we need to study and discover our temperaments.

- **Bring about Personal Transformation**:

Discovering your temperament helps in your personal transformation by dealing with the negative element of your temperament to enhance your personality. It helps in enhancing your personal appeal.

- **Encourage Creativity**:

Information presents us with alternative ways of doing things. To be innovative, we need creative ideas to achieve that. Becoming conscious of our temperament helps us to direct our emotions into positive and creative uses.

- **Give Avenue to Learn**:

It informs us about human characteristic and how they operate in the social environment. It helps us know people's emotional disposition and how to relate to them.

- **Promote Intelligence:**

Intelligence in this context makes us: ingenious, perceptive, and responsible, impactful, skilful, and self-reflective. Your knowledge of temperament enhances your frame of reference. Knowledge is power, ignorance is a disease.

- **Networking:**

Networking is your ability to get connected to people within your organisation and also relate to people external to your group to achieve an aim. Our understanding of temperament helps us connect well, especially with our co-workers, or business associates for personal development.

- **Career Planning and Development:**

Temperament has huge influence on our talents and career selection. In order to choose the kind of career that is most appropriate for you, you need to know your temperament in order to manage your job demands. For instance, Phlegmatics are good managers and negotiators.

- **Success in Relationship**:

Many relationships are on the rock because of emotional dispositions of the partners. Knowing the temperament of your peers, friends, business associates or spouse helps you to manage your emotional differences. It also helps promote team work.

- **Managing Stress**:

Temperament-related stress is not the same as the everyday stress of overwork, or worries over money. It results from the core needs and values of the temperament pattern not being met. Knowledge of your own temperament pattern helps you manage or prevent such stresses.

- **Help Improve on Your Spiritual Life**:

Some people commit sin out of uncontrolled emotions and anger triggered by their temperament. If you know your temperament, it helps you deal with your temperamental emotions and seek support to overcome them.

> *"**G**od could have made us all Sanguines.*
> *We could have lots of fun but accomplish little.*
> *He could have made us all Melancholies.*
> *We would have been organized and charted but not very cheerful.*
> *He could have made us all Cholerics.*
> *We would have been set to lead, but impatient that no one would follow!*
> *He could have made us all Phlegmatics.*
> *We would have had a peaceful world but not much enthusiasm for life.*
> *'He could have made us all Supines.*
> *We would have had best services with affection, but without real decisions.'*
> *We need each temperament for the total function of the body.*
> *Each part should do its work to unify the action and produce harmonious results."*
>
> **Florence Littauer** in her book "The Gift of Encouraging Word," Supine added.

Knowing of temperaments and its implication for life also helps you appreciate social relationship. It helps us see the uniqueness of everybody and appreciate our human diversities better. All temperaments are good for one reason or the other. The only thing that is needed is for us to manage the weaknesses or the shortfalls of our temperaments to enhance our personality.

In the views of Linda V. Berens (2006), knowing our temperament tells us our core needs and values as well as the talents we are more likely to develop. It helps us build our personality, character and draw the admiration of people.

You must note that all the temperaments are good for a purpose or the other, and they all have their positive and negative tendencies. Temperament has much effect on how you relate to people, and how they relate to you. It is important to identify your temperament, develop the strengths and again, deal with the associated imperfections.

CHAPTER THREE

PERSONAL STANDARDS SOCIETY APPRECIATES

Our personality is also influenced by the moral standards or the value system prevailing in the social settings we find ourselves. The values of one society may or may not be accepted in another society. These bring about universal cultural values and cultural relativity. Thus, there are certain values which are universally accepted, while some are limited to social settings; a family, a society or a nation.

The universal values or social standards are moral standards accepted across social settings; family, community, nation and worldwide. For example, honesty and accountability are acceptable at all places; whilst stealing and deceit are wrong everywhere. Relative values are those social standards accepted in one social environment, but not accepted, or without ethical values in another society.

For example, the use of the left hand to show direction is morally wrong in some African societies, while no ethical sensitivity is attached to the use of it in other societies. It is important to note that your personal uprightness or wrongness depends largely on your personal traits, standards, belief system and social setting.

The acceptability or unacceptability of personal values varies from one society to another due to differences in what is accepted or not accepted by the society. Therefore, to be appreciated by a society, you must generally identify and understand the personal and social character traits the society accepts, and the value system or the rules governing the society and abide by them, since these combine to shape your personality.

Ron Kurtus (2007) identifies personality as "the combination of your personal, social and rule-based character traits. Personal character traits concern attitude toward your actions, doing things and achieving goals. Social character traits concern how you deal with other people. Rule-based character traits concern how well you follow your government, cultural and religious laws and rules."

Appreciable societal personality or character traits from Ron Kurtus' perspective can be categorised into Personal character traits, Social character traits and Rule-based character traits, including governmental laws, Socio-Cultural laws and Religious Rules. These characteristics are discussed one after the other.

Personal Character Traits

These are the attitudes you have toward activities. These concern how you react to challenging situations. They are developed from parental training and influence as a young child and through the influence of peers and the social environment. Positive personal traits include:

- Self-confidence, purposefulness, courageousness, carefulness, circumspection, determination, willpower, mental-fortitude and hard work.

They are things you are "supposed to have." Positive personal character traits lead to realisation of your goals and success. They enhance your ability to exhibit reliability. However, negative personal character traits such as cowardice, imprudence, laxity, carelessness, over-confidence, and laziness can lead to failure, frustration or disappointments.

Social Character Traits

Social character traits or moral personality concerns your attitudes and how you deal with other people. Positive social character traits lead to success in relationships and gaining continued rewards. Typical positive social traits include:

- Honesty, kindness, gentleness, reliability, objectivity, trustworthiness, politeness, graciousness, good manners, and being considerate.

They are mostly developed through parental influence; you are told things you are "supposed to do." Thus, they are ingrained without much rational reasoning. For instance, you must show good manners to the elderly. You are not supposed to talk rudely to the elderly. Negative Social Character traits including dishonesty, unreliability, and deceitfulness, result in people's distrust and dislike for you.

Rule-based Character traits

These character traits are prescribed governmental, socio-cultural and religious laws, and rules. A person who obeys these rules and regulations is judged as having good rule-based character. He or she may be considered as law-abiding citizen, a good member of the society or virtuous religious person. Below are some governmental, socio-cultural and religious laws, and rules.

Governmental laws are rules and regulations which are enacted in the form of constitution or a convention to govern a state or country which includes:

- You must not drive over speed limit.
- You must not kill (also a religious and social law).
- You must pay your taxes.

Socio-Cultural laws are customs and traditions which are practiced over the years that become the way of life of the people and are binding on members of the society, this includes:

- You must not marry your own siblings.
- The man is the head of the family.
- As a child you must respect the elderly.

Religious Rules are beliefs and practices of religious groups which are enshrined in a religious book such as the Bible to guide the faithful of the religion. This includes:

- You must not fornicate.
- Honour your parents and the elderly.
- Help the poor and the needy.

Personal character traits concern your attitude towards achieving your aspirations. Social character traits concern how to deal with other people within the social context and Rule-based character traits concern how well you follow governmental, cultural and religious laws and rules.

These rules and regulations are put in place to regulate our interpersonal relationship in the social environment in order to promote harmonious life. Those who abide by these rules are appreciated by society, while those who violate them are considered deviants. Above all, religious rules and norms are there to guide us in our fellowship with our creator and fellow human beings.

Thus, we need to abide by the word of God and use it as our guiding principles. Psalm 1: 1-2 says, "Blessed is the man that walks not in the counsel of the ungodly, nor stand in the way of sinners, Nor sits in the seat of the scornful; But his delight is in the law of the LORD, And in his law he meditates day and night."

If the law of the Lord is your guiding principle, it helps you abide by the progressive governmental, socio-cultural laws, and rules of your society. It shapes your personal character traits, social character traits and rule-based character traits. Again, abiding in the laws of the Lord keeps you from trouble, and assists you to live a worthy and admirable life. Proverbs 25:28 says "Whoever has no rule over his own spirit is like a city broken down, without walls."

To be appreciated by society is not in your ability to please all people, accept all values, beliefs or civilisations, but your ability to identify your persona; who you are within the rules of the society and assume a progressive belief system, in consonance with the will of God; a belief system which motivates and inspires you. Believe in your creator, have principles and identify with like-minded people.

Note that, life needs guiding principles, rules and regulations. What draws you to other people is not only your physical looks or appearance, it is your ability to build a balanced personal and social character traits and play by the rules and regulation of the society. Virtue is doing good to all mankind, abiding by progressive rules and regulations; being good in consonance with the will of God and for the sake of everlasting joy and happiness.

Character is man's greatest need and man's greatest safeguard. It is safer to have good and strong character than very strong and fortified fence wall. Physical looks are important, but not the most important; work on your character traits, value system and play by the rules of society; they shape you for a secure and a better life.

> *Life is guided by principles. Life without principle is life without purpose and life without purpose is life without direction. People of serious minds identify with your personality, principles, and purpose. Your personality reveals who you are, your principles identify your standards for life, within the social setting, and your purpose indicates what you are living for. Believe in your creator, have principles, and identify with like-minded people.*

Apart from abiding by societal ethical values, rules and regulations, you have something special in you which make you unique from other people. This is your personality plus. If you identify and work on your personality plus, it will also enhance your personal appeal. Come with me to explore this together.

CHAPTER FOUR

DEVELOPING YOUR PERSONALITY PLUS

*E*verybody has something good which draws him or her to others no matter how minimal it may be. That is why everybody has a friend, an admirer or can do something unique as a person. All of us have the ability to develop these qualities which are special. This as mentioned earlier, is your personality plus, unique personal strength or charisma, which is mostly used.

The word charisma is from the Greek word "kharisma," meaning "gift" or "divine favour." It is often used to describe the ability to charm or influence people. It refers especially to a quality in people who easily draw the attention and admiration of others due to a "magnetic" quality of personality.

Webster's Ninth New Collegiate Dictionary defines charisma as "a personal magic of leadership arousing special popular loyalty or enthusiasm." It is a quality in people which easily draw the attention and admiration of others due to the 'magnetic' quality of personality. From a general point of view, charisma is a strong personal quality that makes people like you.

Related terms and phrases used to discuss charisma include; grace, exuberance, equanimity, mystique, positive energy, extreme charm, personal magnetism, personal appeal, allure, and many more. Thus, charisma is generally a strong popular personal quality; a personal quality and attractive; it draws people to the charismatic person, it draws followership; it helps the charismatic person draw support from his or her followers; and mostly a catalyst for leadership.

Case Study of Personalities with Special Appeal

When you examine the personality of people with special appeal, it is obvious that they exhibit some unique personal qualities which draw them to people. Let us do case studies of the personality and lifestyle of some legends and their unique characteristics that draw them to people or make them attractive.

Abraham Lincoln: Abraham Lincoln was the 16th President of the US, a man of strong faith, passion and staying power. Lincoln made extraordinary efforts to attain knowledge while working on a farm, splitting rails for fences, and keeping store at New Salem, Illinois, and also studied law privately. He gained a national reputation that won him the Republican nomination for President in 1860 when he debated with Douglas among other things. As President he fought hard and abolished slavery in the United States of America, by issuing Emancipation Proclamation of 1863, which was passed in 1865 into law, after his assassination.

In the face of the civil war of secession, he successfully rallied public opinion through rhetoric and speeches, to maintain the unity of the federation. In a speech during the dedication of the military cemetery at Gettysburg, he declared... "that we here highly resolve that these dead shall not have died in vain-that this nation, under God, shall have a new birth of freedom-and that government of the people, by the people, for the people, shall not perish from the earth."

This was the most moving speech among his many speeches, which also defines democracy. He believes that 'all men, both black and white are born to be free.' He has been consistently ranked by scholars; political historians and public opinion as one of the greatest U.S. Presidents of all time.

 **Mahatma Ghandi:** Mahatma Ghandi was the pre-eminent political and spiritual leader of India, during the Indian independence movement. He was the pioneer of resistance to tyranny through mass civil disobedience, firmly founded upon *ahimsa* or total non-violence which led India to independence from the British and has inspired many movements for civil rights and freedom across the world.

Ghandi spent a number of years in jail in both South Africa and India for his civil right activities. He led nationwide campaigns to ease poverty, expand women's rights, build religious and ethnic amity and increase economic self-reliance. He lived modestly, swore to speak the truth, and undertook long fasts as a means of both self-purification and social protest.

He has been a source of inspiration to leaders such as Martin Luther King Jr., Aung San Suu Kyi of Burma, former U.S. Vice-President Al Gore and the US President Barack Obama. He is honoured in India as the Father of the Nation, his birthday, 2 October, is declared a national holiday, and also declared by UN as the "International Day of Non-Violence" among other numerous honours.

 **Kwame Nkrumah:** Dr. Kwame Nkrumah the first President of the Republic of Ghana is a Pan-Africanist, a great orator, a liberator and visionary leader; he knew how to inspire people for action. His messages such as "Self-government Now" inspired nationalists and the masses of the Gold Coast to work towards the attainment of Ghana's independence.

He was referred to as "Prison Graduate" because he was imprisoned for his liberation activities. He was even in prison for declaring "Positive Action" against the colonialist before he was elected Leader of Government Business in 1951. He believed in the abilities of the black man. He was at the fore front of African liberation struggle for the decolonisation of the Africa continent. At independence, 6th March, 1957, Kwame Nkrumah declared "Ghana's independence would be meaningless unless linked up with the total liberation of the Africa continent."

He had specific messages for specific actions. Though some of his political decisions and strategies were controversial, "he was a visionary leader and years ahead of his compatriot African leaders at the time." In the year 2000, he was rated Africa's personality of the millennium. His birth day has been declared the Founder's Day in Ghana and observed by the African Union throughout Africa.

Margaret Hilda Thatcher: Margaret Thatcher was the Prime Minister of the United Kingdom from 1979 to 1990 and the first woman to lead a major political party in the UK. She entered 10 Downing Street with the determination to reverse the UK's economic decline and to reduce the role of the state in the economy. She was said to need just four hours' sleep a night.

She is considered by many as a revolutionary figure who revitalised Britain's economy, and re-established the nation as a world power. The term 'Thatcherism' came to refer to her policies as well as aspects of her ethical outlook and personal style, including moral absolutism, nationalism, interest in the individual, and an uncompromising approach to achieving political goals.

Her tough-talking rhetoric gained her the nickname the "Iron Lady." Thatcher was awarded numerous national and international honours, including a 'Lady of the Most Noble Order of the Garter,' a Member of 'the Order of Merit,' and 'the Presidential Medal of Freedom,' the highest civilian honour awarded by the United States.

John Fitzgerald Kennedy: John F. Kennedy referred to by his initials JFK, was the 35thPresident of the United States of America. After Kennedy's military service during World War II in the South Pacific, his aspirations turned political, and he was groomed by his father Joseph P. Kennedy, Sr. JFK was elected President in 1960 in one of the closely contested elections in the history of the US.

He was a civil right supporter, orator, a visionary leader and political strategist. He supported racial integration and civil right campaigns. He first announced the goal for landing a man on the Moon. He created the *Peace Corp* for American volunteers to help underdeveloped nations in areas of education, farming, health care and construction.

He was able to forestall the Cold War, Cuban Missile Crisis and the Vietnam War from escalating. He made Americans feel important and needed in building the nation. His famous dictum "Ask not what your country can do for you; ask what you can do for your country" inspired the nation. Despite his relatively short term in office due to his assassination, Americans regularly vote him as one of the best presidents in the history of the US.

 **Martin Luther King Jr.:** Dr Martin Luther King Jr. was an American Clergy, human rights campaigner and prominent leader in the African-American civil rights movement. He raised public consciousness of civil rights movements through his speeches such as "I have a dream" and established himself as one of the greatest orators in U.S. history.

He worked to end racial segregation and racial discrimination through civil disobedience and other non-violent means. He inspired hope for the future. He also paid attention to reducing poverty and opposed the Vietnam War. His main legacy was to secure progress on civil rights and he is referenced as a *human rights icon* today. Nonetheless, King was accused of having "weakness for women."

In 1964, King became the youngest person to receive the Nobel Peace Prize for his work to end racial segregation and racial discrimination. He was also awarded over fifty honorary degrees from colleges and universities among other honours. The Martin Luther King, Jr. Day was established as a U.S. National Holiday in 1986, and observed on the third Monday of January each year in his honour for his human right activism. He is a pacifist and man of peace.

Mother Teresa: Mother Teresa known as Agnesë Gonxhe Bojaxhiu was a Catholic nun who founded the Missionaries of Charity in Calcutta, India; a woman of strong compassion and faith. Fascinated by stories of the lives of missionaries at age 12,she decided to commit herself to a religious life. She devoted her whole life showing mercy and compassion to the dying.

She ministered to the poor, sick, orphan, and dying, whilst guiding the Missionaries of Charity's expansion, first throughout India and then in other countries. She gave hope to the hopeless and the dying. By the 1970s she was internationally famed as a humanitarian and advocate for the poor and helpless. She has been praised by many individuals and governments for her humanitarian activities.

However, she also faced a diverse range of criticism for her methods of administering health care and her belief in the spiritual goodness of poverty. She won the Nobel Peace Prize in 1979 and India's highest civilian honour; the Bharat Ratna, in 1980 for her humanitarian work. Following her death she was beatified by Pope John Paul II and given the title 'Blessed Teresa of Calcutta.'

Nelson Mandela: Mandela was an anti-apartheid activist, the leader of the African National Congress (ANC) and the first post-apartheid President of South Africa. He was convicted on charges of sabotage, while he was leading the military wing of the ANC, *Umkhonto we Sizwe* against apartheid. He served 27 years in prison, spending many of these years on Robben Island.

Nelson Mandela is an enduring spirit and of a strong conviction. He was released from prison on 11

February, 1990; he helped in the transition towards multi-racial democracy in South Africa. He believes in a "democratic and free society in which all persons live together in harmony and with equal opportunities." He is a celebrated elder statesman who voices his opinion on topical issues.

In South Africa he is referred to as *Madiba*, an honorary title adopted by elders of his clan. Mandela has received more than one hundred awards, most notably the Nobel Peace Prize in 1993, Presidential Medal of Freedom of the US and Order of St. John of UK. His birth day 18 July is instituted by the Non-Aligned Movement as a day for voluntary service in his honour. He is a celebrated elder statesman and a world icon; he is a 'Living Legend.'

Oprah Gail Winfrey: Oprah Winfrey is an American media personality, best known for "The Oprah Winfrey Talk Show" and the most watched TV celebrities of all times. Oprah was born into poverty in rural Mississippi to a single mother. She experienced considerable hardship during her childhood, including being raped at the age of nine and becoming pregnant at age fourteen, but overcame all these adversities to become one of the best media personalities in human history.

By the mid-1990s she had reinvented her show with a focus on literature, self-improvement, and spirituality. She is credited with creating a more intimate confessional form of media communication. The show has earned her Multiple-Emmy Awards and is the highest-rated talk show in the history of television. She is also an influential book critic, an Academy Award-nominated actress, and a publisher. Winfrey is very compassionate orator and a people's person. She uses her fame and listening audience to help the less fortunate.

Though criticised for confessional culture on her show, and redefining social norms, she is generally admired all over the world for overcoming adversities to become a benefactor of the under privileged. She has been ranked the richest African American of the 20th century and the most philanthropic African American of all time. She is also considered by many as the most influential woman in the world.

Winston Churchill, a British Prime Minister in the World War II era, was a warrior, historian, writer and a great politician. He was very discerning, steadfast, committed, and courageous leader. He had been among the first to warn about the growing threat of Hitler but, his warnings was largely ignored.

He is noted for his speeches, which were of great inspiration to the British people and Allied Forces. He received a Nobel Prize in Literature in 1953, "for his mastery of historical and biographical description as well as for brilliant oratory in defending exalted human values" He was acclaimed the greatest Britons Leader and one of the most influential leaders in human history.

Dr Esther Ocloo was a Ghanaian industrialist, banker, pioneer of micro-lending, philanthropic, a gender activist, and international leader. She produced innovative solutions to the problems of poverty, hunger and the distribution of wealth in Africa and globally. She was the first chairperson of Women's World Banking, and the founder of the Ghanaian chapter of the International Federation of Business and Professional Women.

She was the first woman to receive the African Leadership Prize for sustainable end of hunger by the hunger project in 1990, among other numerous awards. She was a model to women in Africa and worldwide.

Kofi Annan, the former United Nations (UN) Secretary-General, the first to be elected from the ranks of UN staff, is a reformist, a man of an enduring spirit, and peace maker. He advocates human rights, the rule of law and the universal values of equality, tolerance and human dignity.

The Millennium Development Goals; eight point targets for international development were set up under his administration. He has received honorary degrees from universities all over the world, a Nobel Prize Winner for Peace, as well as a number of awards for his contributions to the aims and purposes of the United Nations. He is one of the greatest diplomats Africa and the world have had.

Ellen Johnson-Sirleaf, the Liberian President and the first democratically elected woman president in Africa is a politician, banker and gender activist. She was married at age 17, but with determination she was able to further her education to the masters' level.

She was a Minister of Finance in Liberia, work with the UN and other international organisations. Johnson-Sirleaf suffered political arrests, exiled and lost presidential election, but went on to win the presidency in 2005. She is nicknamed "Iron Lady" for her fortitude and resilience. She won many awards including Presidential Medal of Freedom, the highest civilian award given by the United States.

Archbishop Benson Idahosa was a Nigerian spiritual leader and a mentor of many ministers of the gospel in Africa and the world over. He worked towards the goal of reaching the unreached in Africa and the rest of the world with the word of God, and ministered in over 123 countries.

He was an accessible leader, a teacher and a man of extraordinary faith. He was a man greatly used by God in his generation. He had a personal charm that endeared him to friends and foes alike.

Miriam Makeba, also known as *Mama Africa* was a South African anti-apartheid activist, and a music icon. She is a singer whose voice stirred up hopes of freedom among millions of South Africans in the anti-apartheid era. She was referred to as "a mother of the anti-apartheid struggle" by Nelson Mandela. In 1965 she won a Grammy Award with Belafonte. She is rated as one of the world's most prominent black African music icons in the twentieth century.

President Nicolas Sarkozy, is an enduring leader with political conviction and hardworking. He is recognised by both his supporters and opponents as a skilful politician and striking orator. He is politically innovative and a reformist.

He pledges to revitalise the French economy, revive work ethics, and minimise intolerance. Even though he is considered by many as controversial, his fortitude, hardworking, and communication skills endear him to both supporters and opponents alike.

Rev. Dr Mensah Anamua Otabil a Ghanaian reverend minister is an outstanding speaker and teacher of the word of God with practicality and inspirations. Even though from low estate with initial challenges of life, he has developed his gifts to the maximum, with exceptional devotion to God, and has affected many lives.

He is a leadership role model, and a blessing to our generation. In fact, he is one of the greatest teachers of the word of God in our time.

Barack Obama, the 44th, and the first African-American US President is a visionary and a reformist. He is a political strategist and an exceptional orator, with extraordinary leadership qualities. His catch word "Yes we can" inspires and gives hope.

Hilary Clinton, former First Lady, State Governor, US Secretary of State and a writer is a unique leader and a speaker in her own right.

From these examples it is obvious that all these personalities, even though they have their personal flaws or weaknesses, they have identified their personal strengths, developed and used them or are using them for the benefit of humanity. They identify some problems of their societies and directed their energy towards solving them. They draw followers and have inspired them for action. Therefore, we can establish from the examples of these personalities that:

- People with personality plus identified their personal qualities and developed them; e.g., Abraham Lincoln, Margaret Thatcher, Nicolas Sarkozy, Oprah Winfrey and all the others discovered their personality plus and developed it. Abraham Lincoln was an orator, enduring, humane and public spirited person, whereas Kofi Annan is an enduring spirit and a man of peace.
- They identify a need and direct their energy towards attaining them; e.g. Abraham Lincoln belief that "all men, both black and white are born

to be free" and worked to abolish slavery in the US. Dr Kwame Nkrumah worked hard to abolish colonialism in Africa and unite the continent, whilst Dr Esther Ocloo worked to reduce hunger in Africa and the world over.

- They have a (vision) message, or catch word; e.g. "Self-government Now" and "Ghana's independence would be meaningless unless linked up with the total liberation of the Africa continent." by Kwame Nkrumah. "I have a dream" by Martin Luther King Jr. John F. Kennedy had a vision of landing man on the moon, and "Yes we can" by Barack Obama. Kofi Annan has helped the UN set up "The Millennium Development Goals."

- They went beyond the average and were quite controversial; e.g. Winston Churchill, Mahatma Ghandi, Margaret Thatcher, Mother Teresa and Martin Luther King Jr. were criticised for their beliefs, decisions or convictions. Oprah's talk show was criticised by some Sociologist such as Vicki Abt for redefining social norms. Winston Churchill was criticised for his handling of British bombing of German city of Dresden in the World War II.

- They have hope and give hope to their followers in the face of challenges; e.g. "Self-government Now" and "Positive Action" by Kwame Nkrumah, "I have a dream" by Martin Luther King Jr. and John F. Kennedy's inaugural address as President inspired the nation for action. Archbishop Benson Idahosa was a hope and inspiration to the church in Africa and worldwide.

- They use communication skills to draw followers; they are mostly orators; almost all people with personal appeal develop and use communication skills as a tool to relate their views; e.g. Margaret Thatcher was nicknamed "Iron Lady" because of her tough-talking rhetoric. Martin Luther King Jr. was famous for his speeches such as "I Have a Dream." Barack Obama is an extraordinary orator.

- They exhibit confidence, courage and much energy; they have staying power, e.g. Mahatma Ghandi, Kwame Nkrumah, Luther King Jr. and Nelson Mandela were all imprisoned for their conviction. In fact, Nkrumah was released from prison to become Leader of Government Business in the Gold Coast, while Nelson Mandela became the first post-apartheid President after 27 years in prison. Rev. Dr Mensah Otabil speaks with conviction, confidence and with an enormous energy.

- Thus, they become popular because they discover their personal qualities, develop them, direct it towards a need, give hope to people and enhance the life of humanity. All of them were either honoured in life or after death for their efforts. Kwame Nkrumah is rated African Personality of the millennium. Oprah Winfrey is rated by many as the most influential woman in the world. Dr Esther Ocloo was recognised by the editorial board of Biographical Publication, England, as one of the Foremost Women of the twentieth Century.

It is noteworthy that everybody has a personal strength or ability, but these qualities need to be developed and directed towards doing something good to the benefit of people. They are in-born, and they are developed in the social environment.

Appealing people largely attract and sustain followership only when they direct their potentials at doing something beneficial to people. In his book "Be a People Person" John C. Maxwell used the word charisma as an acrostic to explain outstanding personal qualities that draw support.

C: Concern -:"The ability to show you care." Charismatic people have the ability to show concern for people's deepest needs and interest. They are more concerned about protecting other people than themselves. To draw people's confidence, you should show honest concern for their needs.

H: Help -:"The ability to reach out." Charismatic people are helpers; they are interested in people's affairs and success. They are not selfish; they are gracious people and they help people to solve their problems. To draw people's confidence, help them to overcome their challenges.

A: Action-:"The Ability to make things happen." They excite people; they are humorous, they are never boring. According to John Wesley "when you set yourself on fire, people just love to come and see you burn." Try to be "Positive Action" person, by doing something beneficial, and people will come around you.

R: Result-: "The Ability to Produce." Charismatic people want to be on the winning side of life. They do not want to win alone; they want other people also to win. They are not self-centred. To be result oriented, discover your strengths, use it to get results, and help others to achieve results.

I: Influence-:"The Ability to Lead. Leadership is influence." If something new or special is happening in your life, you will want to share it. By doing so, you will influence others and they will want to follow you. "What happens through you speaks of your Charisma."

S: Sensitivity -:"The Ability to Feel and Respond." Charismatic people have the ability to be sensitive to changing situations. They take advantage of mood, feeling and spirit of situations. They know how to react to situations. They are discerning, and voice out their concern with courage. To draw people to you, be sensitive to their situations and stand by them in their challenges.

M: Motivation -:"The Ability to Give Hope. The secret of motivating others is providing them with hope." Charismatic people convey hope in precarious situations. To draw people to you, learn problem solving techniques, verbally encouraging and conveying belief in, and support for others.

A: Affirmation -:"The Ability to Build." Charismatic people affirm people for their accomplishments. To affirm others, you need to feel good about yourself and verbally and actively believe in others. People are your only asset. Think the best, believe the best, and express the best in others. Your affirmation will also help play an important part in the personal development of people.

These illustrate some of the very important qualities of people who developed their 'personal magic' and are appreciated by society. They identify their strengths, developed them and put them into good use to the benefit of others. From the illustrations of the personalities with personal appeal and John Maxwell's acrostic exposition, we can establish that, to use your personality plus to draw people to yourself, you should:

- Discover and develop your personality plus.
- Identify a need of your people or society and direct your energy towards it.
- Find alternative solution to the already prescribed solutions to the need.
- Have a vision, dream, message or a catch phrase which inspires you for action.
- Direct your energy towards solving the problem or problems identified.
- Build up your personal confidence and a trustworthy life.
- Develop working relationship with likeminded people.
- Have strong conviction, be quite controversial and go beyond the average.
- Develop your communication skills; learn to speak your thoughts clearly and fluently.
- Genuinely stir up confidence in people, let them know they matter to you so much.
- Never undermine the abilities of other people, even your opponents.

- Keep focused on your vision, never allow yourself to be discouraged when criticised.

I believe charisma or as it were; divine favour is not the preserve of some special people. Everybody has some positive personal strengths; the only thing is that some people's personal appeals are more prominent and more appealing than others.

Everybody has personal strength no matter how minimal it is, you can excel beyond measure, if you believe it, identify it and work on it. Remember, everybody created in the image of God has unique potentials; nobody is created without personal special strengths.

Additionally, work on your communication skills, to be able to bring out what the mind conceives. Whatever the mind conceives, it is the mouth that articulates it. Good communication draws people to you, and character maintains followership. Communication skills are discussed in chapter six.

Barriers to Positive Personality Plus

Barriers to positive personal plus are what John Maxwell refers to as "Roadblocks to Charisma." These are negative and unacceptable character and behavioural traits which put people away from you or are threats to your personal survival. Some of these negative traits are as follows:

- Arrogance, haughtiness, dishonesty, deceit, moodiness, negative mind-set, excessive anger, hatred, corruption, over-ambition, self-centredness, hopelessness, self-petty, despair, dejection, and others.

These characteristics acutely work against your personal appeal. Similarly, if your personality plus is not used properly, they can result in hostile responses. Adolf Hitler was a man of strong charismatic appeal; a great speaker. However, he became a threat to the very existence of the human race. He used his personality plus to prosecute racist agenda, which culminated in the Second World War and his fall.

Some African countries were, and are in conflict because of over-ambition, deceit, arrogance and self-centredness of some of their leaders. Some examples are the 'infamous' Uganda military dictator, Idi Amin Dada, Foday Sankoh, leader of Revolutionary United Front (RUF), Sierra Leone, and Joseph Kony, head of the Lord's Resistance Army (LRA)of Uganda. They projected themselves as genuine leaders and saviours, but later lord it over the people.

> *Everybody has a personal strength, how minimal it is, you can excel beyond measure, if you believe it, identify and work on it. People are drawn to you by your positive personality plus, but unacceptable personal traits and demeanour draw them away from you. Always bear in mind that charismatic people attract and sustain followership mostly, by directing their energy towards doing something good and beneficial for people and society.*

Once again, identify your personality plus and develop it, work on your abrasive personality traits and you will draw many people to yourself. To enhance your personality plus, and feel good about yourself, consciously and genuinely develop positive attitude towards people you come into contact with. This will definitely enhance your personality.

CHAPTER FIVE

DEVELOPING GOOD INTERPERSONAL RELATIONSHIP

*M*ost people look at life from personal point of view only, without much concern for those around them, but very important is that life involves other people in your social environment. Nobody is an island and no individual can live a satisfactory life in isolation; everybody needs somebody. To be admired by others is not only about your personality plus, physical appearance or what you do for yourself, it also includes your interpersonal relationships.

Interpersonal relationship involves a relationship of two or more people, or the ability to create good rapport between yourself and people. Good interpersonal relationship is largely about how you relate to people, your care for others, how you manage your personal, social and rule-based character traits, to create bond of friendship and harmony. It relates to:

- How you care or relate to people.
- How you manage your personal, social and rule-based character traits in relating to people.
- How your relationship benefits you and other people in the social environment.

To build good interpersonal relationship and relate well with people, you must learn to appreciate others. To build attractive personality and positive self-image you must learn to understand and appreciate other people and relate to them well. "A good interpersonal relationship is good bonding with others. It is a relationship that brings understanding, joy and harmony among people."

Interpersonal relationship is about enhancing your positive character traits, appreciating and abiding by the rule of society, fulfilling your "God-given-values," and bringing out the best in you. Let us look at steps to building good interpersonal relationship which I call *Golden Rule Principles of Interpersonal Relationship.* Thus, to have good interpersonal relationship:

Be Peaceable with all People

Be accommodative of all persons as such as possible. If you disagree with other people's views, keep your composure, do not vent your anger, because of differences of opinion. This is also the principle of democracy; agree to disagree. The Bible says in Romans 12:18, "If it is possible, as much as depends on you, live peaceably with all men." In order to be at peace with all people, you should:

- Be tolerant: Keep an open mind at all times. This applies to people and circumstances.
- Be frank in all your manners and speech: Always be straightforward and sincere. Say what you mean and mean what you say.
- Be tactful: Be skilful and gracious in dealing with others as much as possible, in order not to create unnecessary enemies.
- Control your temper: Do not allow your temper to fly; if you do, you will get negative feedback.

Make sure, what you say before two or three people, when collaborated you will not be found wanting. When speaking, get your message across in the shortest possible time, with well-chosen language and diction. If it will be from you, be at peace with all people.

Work on Your Differences with People

Earnestly work as much as possible on every misunderstanding you have with people promptly. Drain off your grievances; do not labour grievances in your heart against people. The bible admonishes; "Therefore, as the elect of God, holy and beloved, put on tender, bearing with one another, and forgiving one another, if anyone has a complaint against another;

even as Christ forgave you, so you also must do." Col 3: 12. Forgive when you are offended by your neighbour, do not pay an eye for an eye. Martin Luther King Jr. said "An eye for an eye will make everybody blind." Biblical preference for resolving conflict is that, when you have disagreement with somebody:

- Go to the person to resolve it one on one, if it fails.
- Call one other person; go to the antagonist to resolve it, if it fails.
- Call on the elders to settle it between you, if it fails.
- Finally, consider the person as an unbeliever.

Take note, once in a while, you will have grievances, or disagreements with people, even your bosom friend. Try to resolve your differences amicably; "the sun should not go down on your anger." If you are at fault, learn to say 'I am sorry;' to say I am sorry does not kill you, it rather re-candle relationships.

Develop a Comfortable Personality that People can Associate with, without a Sense of Strain

Comfortable people are much accommodative, jovial and easy going. According to Norman V. Peale "A comfortable person is easy going and natural." Comfortable natural persons:

- Are sincere: Always be genuine and honest, free from deceit. Be honest as much as possible.
- Express genuine and natural love for everybody they meet, as such as possible.
- Establish satisfactory human relationship with people.
- Have a good sense of Humour: A well developed sense of humour helps you adjust to life's varying circumstances.
- Are flexible: Flexible people are able to adjust quickly to changing circumstances without losing their composure.

If you want people to admire you, you must also develop admiration for others. Some people are by nature likable than others, but a serious attempt to know any individual, will reveal qualities that are admirable and attractive in them.

Acquire the Ability to identify with People's Difficulties or Pain

Identify with people's problems, or difficulties; share in the pains of other people. The unfortunate thing is that some people's day of misfortune becomes some others' time or day of celebration. If you do that, the victim will not be pleased with you. To identify with people's difficulties you must try to:

- Show courtesy; be sensitive and cautious in dealing with people in distress.
- Show people you care when they are in any problem; show genuine compassion towards people.
- Always go out of your way to help others and be kind to them.
- Show concern for people's difficulties in solving their problems.
- Encourage people, if you have no solution to give.

People's misfortune should be a lesson to you, do not add to their pains by making unguarded statements about them. Have a forthright interest in people. If you identify with people's difficulties and help them to overcome them; they will boost your 'self-image.' To be appreciated by people, genuinely try to identify with their problems and be an encouragement to them.

Do not Undermine the Personality of Others

People feel comfortable to talk negatively about how other people look like. They discuss the posture of people, the physical natural looks, to the extent of talking down on people's physical deficiencies. What many do not realise is that nobody has control over natural physical looks and that; everybody has some disability; physical, emotional or the like. To be able to appreciate people without undermining them:

- See all people as the image of God.
- Know that nobody has control over the natural physical looks.
- Keep in mind that, everybody has some form of disability; be it physical, emotional or spiritual.
- Consciously develop genuine warmth for people with disabilities, it is never their fault.
- Remember, physical appearance can change at any time through tragedies like road accident or sickness.
- If people will undermine you and you will not like it, do not do the same to others.

Think of your physical dispositions as a gift of God and use it to enhance the confidence of other people. Princess Diana barring her weakness used her physical disposition to enhance the worth of people through her charities. Appreciate God for your physical disposition, whatever it is, never undermine yourself and never look down upon the physical challenges of other people. To be appreciated, genuinely appreciate everybody whatever their defects.

Help People Boost their Self-image

To draw people to yourself, practice building the 'self' in other people, rather than being egocentric. Make people feel important. Self-centred people are self-seeking and are always ready to cash in on every least opportunity to their advantage. Some people are very self-centred without any respect for the sensitivities of other people. In order to enhance people's ego, you must:

- Develop the habit of appreciating people for their achievements.
- Help people feel good about their successes and achievements.
- Congratulate people on their occasions of success without relating to your personal achievements.

- People's day of achievement or celebration should not be the time to project your "self-importance."
- Show sportsmanship; be gracious in winning and losing. Frankly congratulate your opponents when they do better than you.

If you genuinely elevate the self-respect and personal worth of others, they will naturally appreciate you. Do not be egocentric. Whoever you help to build positive image or self-importance, will give you undying devotion.

Deal with the Scratchy Elements of Your Personality

Scratchy elements of personality are the rough and uncomfortable character traits that draw people away from you. These are irritating personal traits that draw people away from you. Some of them are:

- Irritable tone of voice: indicating that you are in a negative mental state or displeased with someone or something.
- Facial expression while speaking: frowning.
- Overuse of personal pronoun, "I": Use of personal pronoun, "I" becomes irritating and boring if it is overused.

- Exaggerating your personal achievements: Do not blow your own horns too much; let others blow it for you.
- Use of inappropriate choices of words: Learn to use words appropriately.
- Others are gossip, backbiting, cheating, improper dressing etc.

Try to identify conscious and unconscious bad elements of your personality and deal with them. You can frankly identify with a colleague or a counsellor concerning your scratchy character traits and ask them to help you deal with them. Some of these are discussed into more detail under communication skills.

Develop a Deep Spiritual Experience

Develop a deep spiritual connection to your creator. Being connected to your creator would energise you to achieve your vision and mission. The word of God is the source of inspiration which help you encourage people and lift up their spirit. I Timothy 3:16a says, "Without controversy great is the mystery of Godliness." To be spiritually inclined you should:

- Seek God through his word.
- Ask him for direction.
- Inspire yourself with the word of God.
- Take steps of faith, trusting God.

Try the 'God Power' and you will be transformed. Many people are worried; they have even given up on life, because they are disconnected from their creator. Develop deep spiritual experience and the God-given-values in you and you will draw many people to yourself.

What is universally true is that, society demands good social conduct; a virtuous life from us, at all time and we must give just that. Whatever you demand from society, give the same, if not more. Be generous with praise and kind words of encouragement. Say thank you when someone helps you. Make people feel welcome when they come around you.

> *Your physical appearance may draw you to others, but it takes your moral behaviour, emotional disposition, rationality, God-given-values, personal, social and rule-based character traits to build, maintain and sustain admirable and attractive personality. Develop good and deeper relationship with your creator, and always do unto others what you would like them to do unto you.*

John C. Maxwell said, "Life is like a mirror, whatever you give life is what it will give back to you." Your achievements in life depend to a greater extent on how you relate to, and appreciate other people. No individual can live a satisfactory, meaningful and fruitful life in isolation. You must note that:

- Life in the social context is 'give and take.'
  If you want people to respect you,
  'Give respect to others.'
  If you want people to help you,
  'Help those around you, within your ability.'
  And if you want people to honour you,
  'Give honour to whom honour is due.'

Human happiness comes from within to the without. Your true happiness in life lies in you, and with people. You cannot truly be happy, if you make other people sad. Make people feel welcome and happy, when they come around you. Your "welcomes and good-byes" should make people remember, appreciate and associate with you.

CHAPTER SIX

WORK ON YOUR COMMUNICATION SKILLS

Communication is very important in interpersonal relationship and relaying what you think to other people. How you speak is very vital in building your personality and becoming attractive to people. Many people have little knowledge of how to send message without miscommunication, while others dress up without knowing what they communicate. This is mostly because of lack of adequate knowledge of communication and how to use communication skills.

Communication is the process of sending and receiving a message. It can either be verbal or nonverbal. Verbal communication is through the use of speech or word of mouth, whilst nonverbal communication is without the use of speech. Identifying and developing these key skills will also enhance your interpersonal relationship.

Channel of Communication

Words are spoken or written characters that communicate meaning. Their meanings depend on the set of experiences people associate with the words; when one uses them or hear them used. When you are told something before you see it, it has effect on how you feel or think. Thus, your choice of word influences how your listener or listeners perceive you and the message you put across.

Communication, regardless of the communication situation goes through a speech process referred to as Channel of Communication. Channel of communication involves seven elements - speaker, message, channel, listener, feedback, interference, and situation. All these elements interact when you are speaking.

Communication begins with a *Speaker* who relays information in the form of a *Message*. This is whatever you intend to say to the *Listener*; e.g. your friends or an audience. The message goes through a *Channel* in the form of direct speaker-listener, written words, phone call or other channels of interaction. The listener receives the information, *Decodes* it and gives feedback.

Before feedback, the listener filters the message through his *frame of reference*; his total knowledge, experience, goals, values and attitude. This is where many problems arise in communication. Because the speaker and the listener's frame of reference may be different to a larger extent, the meaning of the message cannot always be exactly the same to the listener and the speaker. Therefore, you need to be careful about your language use and expressions.

The listener in the communication situation gives *Feedback* in the form of verbal or nonverbal communication to the speaker, depending on the message received through his or her frame of reference. What the listener receives also depends on the amount of *Interference;* things that impede the communication of the message and the communication *Situation*.

Communication situation is the time and place in which the communication takes place; in the morning or a hot afternoon on the tropics. A one on one situation, public place like a congregation, a general assembly of shareholders, a video conference by chief executives of a Multinational Corporation or a graduation ceremony of graduates of a college. This also includes the lighting system in the room and stage set-ups.

The physical setting and time have much impact on your message. When there is a need for you to choose the communication situation especially, when you want to speak to a love one or special guests, you must consider the impact you want to make, before you decide the communication situation.

Using Words in the Communication Situation

When you are speaking to people, you must observe the communication situation and make sure that you speak to the hearing of your listeners, whether in the formal or informal situation. You must also use words well to carry your intended message to your audience. Words have two kinds of meaning - denotative and connotative.

The denotative meaning of a word is the literal or dictionary meaning of words or phrases. It is the precise, literal and objective meaning of words. Connotative meaning on the other hand is the meaning suggested by association or emotions triggered by a word or phrase. It is variable, figurative or subjective meaning. In simple terms, connotative meaning is the applied meaning of the word. To use language or word to carry the right or the intended information and meaning, work on the following:

- Try to understand the meaning of words you use as much as possible. Choose words skillfully for their denotative and connotative meanings.
- Use words accurately and correctly. If you are not sure of the meaning of a word, look up the meaning

in a dictionary; if possible find the origin of the word, it will guide you to use it correctly.

- Learn the correct pronunciation of words and articulate them accurately. The dictionary can help you achieve this. This is essential because there are words which sound similar, and if not uttered well, it will carry the wrong meaning and create confusion in the mind of your listeners.

- Make your language vivid and interesting by using imageries and rhythms. You can generate imageries by using concrete words, similes and metaphors. Your pattern of articulation, repetition of words; assonance and alliteration make rhythms which enrich your language.

- Use words appropriately. Use words to suit the occasion and the level of your listeners. Do not try to impress people so much by using words out of context or words your listeners will find very difficult to understand.

Very important to note is that words or language is used in a social situation with audience diversities. According to Brydon and Scort (1994), audience diversity is "the cultural, demographic, and individual characteristics that differ among audience members." All these diverse orientations influence the communication situation and how your listeners relate to you and what you relay to them.

Diversities of individuals in the communication situation such as language differences, personal views on issues, meaning of gender issues, value system, social status, religious and political orientations affect how people respond to you. To communicate well, learn the relationships between language and diversities, especially cultural diversities, because these affect your communication and how people perceive you.

Avoid unnecessary use of sexist language and use more of nonsexist language. Sexist language such as "you are only a woman" stereotypes women on the basis of gender, but nonsexist language such as "you are only human" prevent stereotyping people based on gender. I am not saying do not use words which differentiate gender, but minimize its use. Remember your words and phrases influence the meaning of your message in the mind of people and how they perceive and respond to you.

Demosthenes noted that "A vessel is known by the sound, whether it be cracked or not; so men are proved, by their speech, whether they be wise or foolish." Be cautious about what you say at any time and place, and be careful about unguarded statements.

"The tongue of the wise uses knowledge rightly, but the mouth of fools pours forth foolishness."Proverbs 15:2. Do not speak when you are annoyed or upset, if you do, you will regret, you did. I tell people 'if you want to make the most regrettable statement in life, speak when you are annoyed.'

Let your words be guarded, your listeners are the witnesses to whatever statement you make, whether guarded or unguarded. At any place or time, if you have nothing to say, abstain or desist from speaking. Whatever you say today, would find you out tomorrow. Whenever you meet people or talk to them on the phone, take note of your welcomes or opening statements, closing remarks or good-byes. They mostly live indelible marks on the mind of people about you. A wholesome tongue is like a tree of life, it produces good fruits and the fruits are shared in joy.

When communicating with people on the phone, be careful about your opening statements, what you discuss, choice of words, and closing remarks, because you do not know the frame of mind or the intentions of the person you are talking to, or the kind of phone being used to receive the call. In fact, we are in a world or era of sophisticated technology where people can tap your voice on the phone. If you are not careful about what you say on the phone your abrasive and unguarded statements may be tapped or recorded and use against you one day.

When you have a radio or a television on, close to you before you speak on the phone, minimise the volume or turn off the sound completely. Otherwise, you will get feedback from the radio or television, which will interfere with or impede the communication process. Always listen carefully before you communicate with people on the phone to avoid miscommunication.

Misconceptions of About Language and Culture

Very important and relevant to the discussion of language is how you relate to people in a bilingual or a multilingual environment; an environment where two or more languages are spoken. Some people have the misconception that their language is superior to the languages of others, thus, considering some other languages as inferior.

Nonetheless, there is no evidence in Linguistics to give credence to this conception. Language is for communication of ideas; a medium of expression in daily transactions and nothing else. When two or more people meet and they can transact their business in whatever language; communication has taken place and language has perform its function.

Why people conceive of superiority of language is because of how popular the language is at a particular time, the number of people who speak it, and how simple or easy it is to learn and speak the language.

Nevertheless, how widespread a language is or the number of people who speak it does not make it superior and make other languages inferior. To relate well to people and promote multilingual and cultural harmony:

- Look at, and treat all languages as medium of expression and communication.
- Do not belittle any language, because if people undermine your language you will not like it.
- Appreciate all languages and do not denigrate anybody because of the language he or she speaks.

Take note that almost all people have emotional attachment to their culture, and language which is a component of culture, and most people rise to the defense of their culture, when it is undermined. Never make derogatory remarks of people and their language and do not get yourself involved in conflict over language, it serves no better purpose. Rather make efforts to learn a phrase or two in other languages, when in a multicultural environment, this will endear you to people from other cultures.

Avoid ethnocentric or racist language when speaking to people, if you want to attract admirers across cultures and stay away from conflict. Ethnocentrics belief that their group or culture is superior to all other group or cultures, whilst racists rate their colour pigment superior to others.

These are mistaken notions and unnatural; they even demonstrate your ignorance or lack of knowledge of humanity. Learn to respect and appreciate all languages and cultural diversities; it enhances your personality and cosmopolitan image.

Nonverbal Communication

In verbal communication, you enhance your speech or otherwise, by your bodily expressions, which interplay with your speech to convey message. This is referred to as Non-verbal Communication (NVC).Lucas E. Stephen (2001), a communication expert, defines nonverbal communication as "communication that occurs as a result of appearance, posture, gesture, eye contact, facial expression, and other nonlinguistic factors." It is the process of communication through sending and receiving messages without the use of words or speech.

Nonverbal or bodily behaviour in human communication helps us to: express emotions, convey interpersonal attitudes, to accompany speech in managing the cues of interaction between speaker and listeners, self-presentation of one's personality and daily formalities.

Research has shown that body language impacts communication process by 55%, tone of voice 38%, and word takes only 7%. These show that most of our communication is nonverbal. Nonverbal communication includes eye contact, facial expressions, gestures, posture, proximity, and tone of voice, also known as paralanguage.

Eye Contact

Eye contact, is an important channel of interpersonal communication, it helps regulate the flow of communication. And it signals interest in others. Eye contact can convey:

- Passion, signal when to talk, finish, or aversion.

Speakers, who make eye contact with their audience, open the flow of communication and convey interest, concern, warmth and credibility. The frequency of eye contact may suggest either interest or boredom.

Facial Expressions

The human face is able to express countless emotions without saying a word. A smile, frown, raised eyebrow, yawn, and sneer all convey information. Facial expressions continually change during interaction with others and are monitored constantly and decoded by your audience. A facial expression among others is a powerful cue that transmits:

- Happiness, surprise, fear, sadness, disgust, affection, dislike, attachment or hatred.

Thus, if you smile frequently you will be perceived as more likable, friendly, warm and approachable. A frown on your face may put off your audience or listener(s). My caution is that; make sure your facial expressions correspond with your intentions to avoid miscommunication through facial expressions. Facial expressions are almost the same across cultures.

Gestures

One of the most frequently observed, but least understood, cues is a hand movement. Most people use hand movements regularly when talking. If you fail to gesture while speaking, especially to a group of people, you may be perceived as boring, stiff or unanimated. Gestures include:

- Use of the hand to wave, point or beckon, and nodding or shaking the head sideways when speaking.

Lively and dynamic gestures capture attention and provide entertainment. Make sure your gestures bring out the right expression and meaning. Note that the meaning of gestures varies across cultures, and regions, so it is important to be careful to avoid misinterpretation of your gestures.

Proximity

Proximity is the study of how people use and perceive the physical space around them. The space between the sender and the receiver of a message influences the way the message is interpreted. Space in nonverbal communication according to Scott Mclean can be divided into four main categories:

- Intimate, social, personal, and public space.

You can also use physical space to communicate many different nonverbal messages, including signals of dominance, authority, friendliness or affection. The perception and use of space varies significantly across cultures, and different levels, and settings within cultures.

Paralanguage

Paralanguage or tone of voice is the nonverbal cues of your voice. These nonverbal speech sounds provide delicate, but powerful clues into your true feelings and what you really mean. This nonverbal communication includes such vocal elements as:

- Tone, pitch, rhythm, timbre, loudness, and inflection.

For maximum effect, learn to vary these elements of your voice. Tone of voice, for example, can indicate sarcasm, anger, affection, or confidence.Without variation of the vocal elements, listeners perceive you as boring or dull.

The most significant thing to note from this is that, voice is important, not just as the conveyer of the message, but also as a complement to the message. As you communicate, you should be sensitive to the influence of tone, pitch, and quality of your voice on the interpretation of your message by the receiver(s). Try to modulate your voice while speaking in order not to be tagged as boring.

Posture and Body Orientation

You communicate several messages by the way you walk, talk, stand and sit. For instance, standing erect, but not rigid, and leaning slightly forward communicates to your audience that you are:

- Sociable, approachable, accessible and friendly.

Interpersonal closeness results when you and your audience face each other. Speaking with your back turned to your audience or looking at the floor or ceiling should be avoided. It communicates lack of interest or unpreparedness to your listeners.

We also communicate a great deal through touch. Think about the messages given by the following: a firm handshake, a timid tap on the shoulder, a warm bear hug, a reassuring pat on the back, a patronising pat on the head, or a controlling grip on your arm.

In addition to the above, your movement; backward and forward, side by side, vertical, and others, communicate nonverbally to your audience. For example when your movement is monotonous, it is an indication that you do not have command over your subject, shy or you are overcome by stage fright. Work on these skills to improve your communication. Listening is also a very crucial issue of communication, which affects interpersonal relationship; it is discussed in the next chapter.

Appearance as a Nonverbal Communication

Earlier, I pointed out that your physical looks may be good, but it is not the only thing that draws people to you. Nevertheless, your personal appearance is part; and affects your total personality. The only caution is that you should not put too much emphasis on your appearance, while you forget your inner personality and character. How you present yourself to the public speaks volume about whom you are and affects your interpersonal relationship.

Personal appearance is generally defined by the way we groom or dress ourselves and is commonly influential in how other people form opinions about us. It is obvious therefore that, care should be given to how you appear in order to make the best and intended impressions.

Your way of dressing, hairstyle and makeup communicate non-verbally about you, and different people interpret it differently with their frame of reference or cultural orientation. This is also referred to as object communication. This includes among other things clothing, hairstyles, accessories and makeup. Appearance in the public view can be measured in two ways:

- The impression people first create about you, when you appear in a particular way; your clothing, accessories, and hairstyle communicate your ideals to people.
- How you perceive yourself as a result of your dressing and the impact it makes on your self-confidence.

According to a communication expert Dela Leathers, "Our visible self-functions to communicate a constellation of meanings which define who we are and what we are apt to become in the eyes of others." The others include the people you come into contact with. If the impression you intended to make by your dressing contradicts the impression you create in the mind of people, it can affect your self-confidence and respect.

If people perceive you as well dressed, they also to a larger extent perceive you as smart, sociable and confident. It can also boost your personal confidence. Research has shown that people who feel their appearance is appreciated by the public enjoy greater self-confidence than those who feel their appearance is not appreciated.

You have no control over body type and height, but you have maximum control over your clothing, hairstyle and makeup, and you can do something about it. Appearance has significant effect on the perception of people around you. Interpretation of clothing, hairstyles, and accessories vary from one society to another. Note that you never get a second chance to make a first impression on people you meet for the first time.

You should also cultivate cleanliness and neatness of body and clothing. Work on your personal hygiene; your nails, body odour and breath. Before you put up a look for an occasion, a meeting or any social gathering, inform yourself of the occasion and dress code. Try to dress simple and attractive as much as possible; do not expose 'your vital statistics.'

The most unfortunate thing about appearance is that you may have inner character, but if you do not know how to present yourself in public, you will misrepresent yourself. Before you attend an occasion, get yourself informed of the dress code.

Appearance they say is deceptive, so you need to appreciate your look before you go out. Do not follow every fashion; some fashions take away your very dignity and respect. 'All that glitters is not gold and remember there is no art of finding the minds construction in the face.' Some fashions create the wrong impressions about you.

> *Your communication; verbal and non-verbally; body-language and appearance speak so much about you. They have significant effect on how people perceive and appreciate you; different people interpret them differently with their frame of reference and socio-cultural orientations. Be mindful of your speech and body language, try to dress simple and attractive as much as possible; do not expose 'your vital statistics.'*

Good use of language; words and expressions, is one very important means of drawing people to yourself.

People admire good orators who are able to communicate their thoughts and send the right message to their listeners. Orators like Martin Luther King Jr., Jesse Jackson, Patrick Lumumba, and Barrack Obama, are able to draw people to themselves through good communication skills apart from their humanitarian activisms.

The French President Nicolas Sarkozy is able to draw much attention, admiration and support from both supporters and opponents, because of how eloquent and coherent he speaks, apart from his passion and hard work. US Secretary of State Hillary Clinton is admired by many people, because of her command over language and public speaking arts. You should use words appropriately and learn the nonverbal skills to enhance your communication skills.

Your ability to understand and use verbal and nonverbal communication skills is a very powerful tool that will help you connect with others, express what you really mean, and build better relationships. Your knowledge of these forms of communication and others will help you correct or improve on your communication skills and social appeal.

CHAPTER SEVEN

SIX-L RULES OF DRAWING
PEOPLE TO YOURSELF

Being attractive is more than your physical appearance or attraction, and how you communicate. It is more than your clothing, hairstyle and accessories. Lisa Weseman asserts that "With so much time and money devoted to being physically attractive, it's easy to forget that being attractive is so much more than looks." He points out that, to draw people to yourself, you must listen to people, learn about things around you, live interesting life and love other people.

Additionally, to draw people to yourself, you do not only listen to them, learn about things around you, live interesting life and love other people, you should also long (desire) to see others achieve their purpose and lead a life that people will like to identify with, and follow. These I call Six-L Rules of Drawing People to Yourself.

The *Six-L Rules* concept is an idea derived from *Issues of Life* which starts with the alphabet "L" that affect personality and interpersonal relationships. These are to Listen, Learn, Long, Live, Love, and Lead.

Thus, the Six-L Rules states that to bring out the best in you and draw people to yourself: Listen and pay attention to people; Learn to seek knowledge of your world; Long to be a solution to people's problems within your ability; Live a life which is attractive and beneficial to people; Love people as they are and be selfless; and Lead a life that is exemplary and worth associating with. Let us discuss the Six-L Rules one after the other.

Listen: Listen and pay attention to people.

Listening is the process of receiving, attending to and assigning auditory as well as visual and tangible stimuli. You need to be an active listener; conscious and responsive in the communication process. You should listen in order to understand, to appreciate and be critical about the facts presented. To be a good listener, you should:

- Make eye contact with the speaker.
- Tune up your mind to the speaker.
- Make positive body expressions that show you are listening.
- Make sure you comprehend what has been communicated.
- Follow up with a contribution or a question, when necessary.

- Avoid attacking the personality of the speaker when you disagree with him or her.

Be a good listener to people when they are talking to you; pay attention when people are talking to you or when listening. James 1:19 says "let every man be swift to hear, slow to speak." In order to listen effectively, listen for main ideas, listen for significant details, and learn to draw suitable inferences. Do not pretend to be listening, while actually your mind is on another person or something else.

In the view of Weseman "listening to people makes them feel interesting and attractive - feelings that they will begin to associate with you." How do you feel when you are talking to somebody and the person's attention is drawn to somebody or something else? A famous writer once said "the greatest gift you can give to the other is the purity of your attention." If you need people's attention, give them your attention.

Learn: Learn to seek knowledge about your world.

Learning is an experience that has formative effect on the mind, character and physical ability of the individual. You need to learn about the things you are interested in and have command over your area of study and profession. Read about your role models, historical figures and events, the word of God, novels and current affairs. To enhance your learning ability and knowledge:

- Cultivate the habit of reading.
- Regularly visit the library or browse the internet to collect information.
- Read news items and books that give you dispassionate and diverse information.
- Develop your belief system; religious, political or socio-cultural ideas and get informed about other world views.
- Have discussion with friends who are open minded for divergent views to improve your knowledge.
- Express your views dispassionately without looking down upon those who disagree with your point of view.
- Seek intellectual opinion or advice from experts, experienced and level headed people when necessary.
- Learn to make a difference, be controversial sometimes, and learn not to please all people, at all times.

If you develop the habit of learning or studying, not only will you make yourself happier, you will also become more knowledgeable and passionate about the world around you, creating a fascinating and exciting atmosphere around yourself.

Note: I am not suggesting you become 'jack of all trade,' but rather get yourself informed about the world around you. Knowledge rules the world; knowledge is power. Mind you, "The mind is a terrible thing to waste."

William Feather noted that "education is being able to differentiate between what you do know and what you do not know. It is knowing where to go to, find out what you need to know; and it is knowing how to use the information once you get it." Acquire knowledge and use it to better the lots of people and yourself. Knowledge abounds in the world, but ignorance permeates society. Seek knowledge and understanding, and let wisdom be your friend.

Long: Long to be a solution to people's problems within your ability.

To long for something is to want it very much or strongly desire it. There are diverse desires, but your desires to be a solution to people's problems make them appreciate you. Have a strong desire to be a solution to people's predicaments within your means or ability. By doing so you are even bringing out the best in yourself. People should not be the means to your end; they should be an end in themselves. In order to bring out the best in yourself:

- Desire the best for people.
- Give support to people within your abilities.
- Believe in yourself and get people to believe in themselves.
- Let people benefit from your vision and mission.
- Your vision should be 'People Vision,' do not be self-centred.

The most popular people are not people who are self-centred, but those who desire the best for others. The world's most popular people are those who desire the best for others. The most popular people in history are for example, people who liberate their people from difficulties or satisfied the needs of others. Abraham Lincoln is a world icon today, because he among other things fought to abolish slavery and even paid the price with his life.

Kwame Nkrumah of Ghana is Africa's most popular personality for the twentieth century and Africa's personality of the millennium, because, he endeavoured to liberate Africa from colonialism. Archbishop Idahosa of Nigeria was looked up to by many religious leaders in Africa and the world over, because of his dedication to the things of God and also helping many to discover and fulfil their calls. Your desire to do something good for people endears you to them. It makes people admire and associate with you.

Live: Live a life which is attractive and beneficial to people.

The most attractive people are those who live interesting and fulfilling lives. They make the effort to live for a purpose or a course. Your purpose should not be how to live a comfortable life alone; live a broad base life with a purpose which will be beneficial to people. Live for a purpose that you will find it difficult to give up on. To live an interesting and fulfilling life, that will attract many people to you:

- Live your life to please your creator: He has sent you on a mission on earth.
- Live your life with purpose: Your purpose brings meaning and fulfilment to your existence.
- Live your life with principles: Your principles shape and illuminate your direction.
- Live your life to affect your generation; your family, your society, your country or humanity at large:

You are created for the pleasure of God and the people around you, your generation needs you.

Make frantic efforts to live a fulfilling life; a life which is meaningful and beneficial to others. Oprah Winfrey is admired all over the world by most people not because of her wealth, but because of her philanthropic work and more intimate media form of communication which is human centred and problem solving. She lives and pursues her life purpose and dream which is beneficial to many, especially the vulnerable and the needy.

Having a broad range of interests, make you more exciting and appealing. You will end up meeting very prominent people with whom you have things in common. But in all things, place God first. "Seek ye first the kingdom of God, and his righteousness; and all these things shall be added unto you." Matt 6: 33. Seek ye not bread and gold, but seek a life that is pleasing to your creator and beneficial to others, bread and gold will come naturally.

Love: Love people as they are and be selfless.

The most fascinating people who others will want to be around are also those who genuinely love people.

They live selflessly and always try to show love to people. They lead ordinary lives, but never cease to do extraordinary things. For instance, Mother Teresa devoted her whole life showing mercy and compassion to the under privilege and the dying and draws many admirers to herself. In order to show genuine love to others:

- Do not discriminate against, or undermine people.
- See every human being as an image of God.
- Make conscious effort to approach life with a loving heart and attitude.
- Find opportunities to show genuine love to people.
- Do favour to people without expecting payback from them.

Henry Ward Beecher once said that "No one can deal with the hearts of men unless he has the sympathy which is given by love.... you must have enough benevolence, not only for yourself, but for others, to pervade and fill them. This is what is meant by living a Godly life." Love is the doorway through which the human soul passes from self-centredness to selflessness and from isolation to fellowship with all mankind. Jesus demonstrates his love for us through his death that, "whosoever believes in Him will not

Six-L Rules Of Drawing People To Your Yourself

perish, but have everlasting life."Our lives must be a demonstration of the love of God to our neighbours.

By taking the focus off yourself, and loving people for whom they are, you will begin to assume a warmer, more giving nature that will make other people want to be around you. And even better, you just might find yourself drawn to a whole new world of unique and interesting people. Your generosity and kindness to people, makes them love you back. Love all and be without malice for anyone. You must also love what you do, for it to become beneficial to people and rewarding to you.

Lead: Lead a life that is exemplary and worth associating with.

Lead in this context means to live an exemplary life that people will like to identify with or follow. It is the root word of the word 'leader' meaning leading by example. Those who truly lead lives that are exemplary attract followership. They attract followers, because their lifestyle is well structured with good moral principles worth identifying with. To lead a life that will attract people to you:

- Evaluate and work on your lifestyle.
- Plan your life and lead your life with values.
- Develop qualities that attract followership.
- Do not undermine the qualities or personality of other people.
- Try to be a source of inspiration to people by encouraging them, through words and action.

The kinds of people who relate to you depend on how you live your life. It is said: "Birds of the same feathers flock together." Do not expect people of virtue to identify with you, if you do not live a life that meet their standards. People come around you sometimes not to keep your company instantly, but to study and know who you are. Your character speaks for itself; it either draws people to you or draws them away from you.

Everybody writes his or her own life testimony. Sometimes people may say something which may not be true about you. However, mostly your own actions and inactions generate inconclusive stories and opinions about you. Lead a simple and straightforward life with guiding principles which will minimise unsubstantiated stories and opinions about you. Everything you do people will talk about you, just try to do the right thing, that even, if people fabricate stories and unfair opinions about you, your good deeds will vindicate you. The best kind of life speaks for itself; it produces reliable and committed followership; who are ready to defend your name, reputation and integrity in all situations.

> *To draw people to yourself, develop the ability of Listening to people; Learn about your world, Live interesting and attractive life which is beneficial to people; Long to help people within your ability; Love people genuinely and for who they are; and Lead a life that is worthy of emulation. To rise to the top, it is people who push you up. Even though it takes personal efforts to achieve your vision, you always need people around you and the help of God to achieve your potentials and purpose.*

In life, there are 'push and pull factors,' so you must be careful about how you relate, and deal with people. People can push you up, and they can pull you down also. Bear in mind, to be promoted in every human endeavour; at school, at work, appointment or election to any higher office, you need the support of people. You need recommendations and support, if not from those above your status; it may be from those below your status.

How To Build Attractive Personality

Man is always in the social environment, you influence people's life, and people affect your life, either directly or indirectly, positively or negatively. Be careful about how you deal with everybody who comes your way, either at home, at work; in every moment of socialisation. Do not lord yourself over people, just because of your title, office or social status.

Going up you need people, maintaining the top you need people, your coming down too people contribute to it. "Everybody needs somebody at every time and situation." Bear in mind that sometimes the person you see as "A Know body" today will be the person you need tomorrow, to get to the top and maintain the top. Show respect to everybody, whatever their abilities or inabilities; you will need them one day.

CHAPTER EIGHT

BUILDING PERSONAL CONFIDENCE
AND TRUSTWORTHY LIFE

*P*ersonal confidence is very vital in drawing support. If you do not have confidence in yourself or your abilities, do not expect anybody to have confidence in you. Confidence is the belief that you are able, or you have the ability to do something.

A person who is confident believes in his or her capabilities. To be attractive you need to build your confidence level. Confidence helps you believe in yourself, and other people when necessary. Two Bible texts which are my sources of inspiration and confidence boosters in everything I do are:

A Psalm of David which says; "The LORD is my light and my salvation; whom shall I fear? The LORD is the strength of my life; of whom shall I be afraid? When the wicked came against me to eat up my flesh, my enemies and foes, they stumbled and fell. Though an army may encamp against me, my heart shall not fear; though war should rise against me, in this I will be confident." Psalm 27:1-3

As Paul said; "I know how to be abased, and I know how to abound. Everywhere and in all things I have learned both to be full and to be hungry, both to abound and to suffer need. I can do all things through Christ who strengthens me." Philippians 4: 12-13.

God created us in his own image, and transferred into us his abilities. His word; the Rhyma of God, unearth confidence in us when we read, meditate and internalise it. You can do every good thing possible and deal with your fears, when you have the word of God; the God Power. To build your confidence Level:

- Have confidence in the power of God; your strength comes from the Lord who makes heaven and earth.
- Find your interest areas of life and develop them to the maximum.
- Look beyond your sources of fear, focus on God, your potentials and purpose.
- Recount your earlier achievements and they will urge you on, never focus on your challenges.
- Develop a critical mind and the ability to evaluate situations and take decisions.
- Get the right information when you want to speak to an issue and speak with courage.
- Develop friendship with confident people and stay away from those who undermine your abilities.
- Take constructive criticisms in good faith, they should not demoralise you.

According to John Maxwell *"confidence is contagious."* It draws people to you. You cannot give what you do not have. You cannot attract people to yourself or impact them, if you do not have self-confidence and courage. Believe in yourself and you will turn more of yourself into practical use and become influential. Develop confidence in your creator, those around you who merit your confidence, and have confidence in your abilities.

Winston Churchill is regarded as one of the greatest and admirable political leaders of the United Kingdom, and in political history by most political analyst for his steadfast commitment, confidence and courageousness. With his steadfast commitment to the cause of liberty, confidence and courage, his nation was protected from external aggression.

Rev. Dr Mensah Otabil is admired by many in Ghana, and regarded as role model, because of how he teaches the word of God with confidence, practicality and inspirations. He has developed his gift to the maximum, with extraordinary devotion to God, and has affected many lives.

You can also do extra-ordinary things and draw many people to yourself, if you have confidence in the power of your creator and your abilities.

Enemies of Self-Confidence

Many people are not able to display self-confidence because they make friend with what l call enemies of self-confidence. Some of the enemies of self-confidence are:

- Inferiority complex; feeling of personal inadequacies or shortfalls.
- Timidity; shyness, without boldness to stand the presence of other people.
- Making unnecessary comparisons; rating other people higher than yourself.
- Negative mind-set; seeing every challenge as impossibility and insurmountable.
- Ignorance and illiteracy; lack of facts or lack of knowledge of issues around you.

To avoid these enemies of self-confidence, work on yourself to overcome them. In fact, they are confidence killers. Always note that you have the ability to rise above every negative self-image. Whatever the mind conceives regularly may have impact on your abilities. Identify your strengths and develop them, and work on your weakness so as to overcome them.

Stop comparing yourself to other people, you are also a unique image of God, you are not a replica of anybody to keep undermining yourself, because of somebody's strengths or positive self-mage. Avoid negative mind-set, get knowledge and learn to speak and do things with confidence.

Look at yourself with a positive mind light and you will see yourself doing many wonderful things. Nevertheless, I am not suggesting to you positive thinking without action. Mind you: positive thinking is good, but positive thinking without action; determination, hard work, devotion and faith in God, is hallucination; it is day dreaming and a figment of your imagination. Think positive, have confidence and be an action person.

Empty yourself of negative self-image. When you project confidence and self-assured attitude with hard work, you are telling others that you merit their respect, confidence and support. Be poised for 'positive action' with confidence and you will turn yourself into a magnetic force; attracting positive minded people to yourself.

Fill yourself with positive mind-set; inhale confidence, and exhale timidity and lack of self-respect. To become a person of honour or a person people look up to, is not achieved on a silver platter. It takes concerted efforts, consistency, perseverance, and confidence, willpower and trust in God to achieve it.

Building Trustworthy Personality

A very important trait that gets people close to you, and maintains relationship is trust. To trust somebody is to believe that, the person is honest, fair and reliable. Trust is a very vital ingredient which strengthens and preserves relationship. In order to build trust:

- Be slow to speak, let your words be few in order not to contradict yourself when speaking.
- Do not exaggerate your personal accomplishments; your actions should speak louder than your words.
- Always remember "people's secrets are their life and your secret is your life." Learn to keep people's personal secrets, and corporate secrets, when necessary.
- If you know when you are in the company of some people, they could intimidate you to speak to whatever you do not want to talk about, please live them or break their company.
- Know you cannot please everybody; to please everybody is to please nobody.
- Your yes should be yes, and your no should be no; do not 'easily for go' your stand on issues and values.

- Be satisfied with what you have achieved at a time and inspire yourself to do more.

Build your confidence without using the sensitivities of other people to boost your image. Some people think when they backbite or reveal secretes of others, it will make people like them and make them popular. This is not true; backbiting will rather make people shun your company, when they get to know you are a gossip or a rumourmonger. Learn to keep people's affairs in trust for them as much as possible.

Remember, "Good name is better than riches." Riches are good, but riches cannot buy good name. Some people with inferiority complex especially, think that in order to boost their self-respect or enhance their image, they have to belittle other people. If you have that attitude, please desist from it, because it will rather destroy the little respect that you might have earned.

George Macdonald once said "To be trusted is a greater compliment than to be loved." People's love for you may grow and endure; if they know you are trustworthy, but when they realise you are not reliable their love for you will fade away or even die off. Many people lost very great opportunities in life including jobs and promotions, because they cannot be trusted,

How To Build Attractive Personality

while some relationships are on the rocks because of mistrust. Why some people cannot be trusted is that they:

- Easily betray trust; they easily let out people's affairs and corporate secrets.
- Cannot keep promises; they easily fail their promises and vows to people.
- Want to please everybody; they want to relay secrets of people to get favours or to boost their self-worth.
- Cannot control their mouth; they have 'watery mouth.'
- Do not have standards or principles guiding their life and relationships.
- Consider other people as a means to their end; they do not care about the feelings of other people.
- Cheat people to enhance their wealth; they are exploitative, selfish and self-seeking.
- Feel so superior to other people; they consider other people as inferior to them.

What worries me so much is when I promise and failed. It affects my emotion and I even have headache sometimes. When I am able to fulfil my promise, it is like a heavy load lifted from my head. How do you feel when you break trust? You need to build up a trustworthy personality to maintain your relationships and social appeal. This also has to do with conscience; develop good conscience, keep trust, and do not allow your conscience to die.

Build a trustworthy life by keeping your word to people. Galsworthy said "Honesty of thought and speech and written word is a jewel, and they who curb prejudice and seek honourably to know and speak the truth are the only builders of a better life." If you want to build and have a better life, never compromise your principles. Speak when the need be, keep quiet, if you have nothing to say.

Charles Lindbergh on his part said "Spiritual truth is more essential to a nation than mortar to its cities' walls. For when the actions of a people are unguided by these truths, it is only a matter of time before the walls themselves collapse." Trust is like a defence wall; the more you keep it, the more you are fortified, if you break trust, it will crumble your personality and personal respect.

> **D**o not compare yourself to people in any way, you are a unique image of your creator, you are not a replica of anybody to keep undermining yourself because of people's strengths or positive self-mage. Look at yourself with positive mind light and you will see yourself doing many wonderful things. Identify your strengths and develop them, work on your weaknesses to enhance your self-confidence and keep a trustworthy life.

It is very unfortunate that many people including the elderly, who should be gatekeepers of morality, throw honesty and trust to the dogs. But, I desire a generation in which truth will be upheld and rewarded, rather than a world which uphold dishonest and distrusted people and reward them, because they are connected to "the Big Men" as in some parlance.

Build up a good moral principle, never sell it. Build up your confidence level and be honest in all situations as much as possible. Live up to your words; sincerity leads to mutual trust. When you are trustworthy, you often attract many positive relationships.

CHAPTER NINE

CONCLUSION AND INSPIRATIONAL MESSAGE

*B*uilding attractive and admirable personality should be through conscious efforts and self-assessment. To improve on your temperament, personal traits, societal and ethical values, working on your personality plus, being at peace with all people, dealing with your scratchy attitudes, developing deep spiritual experience, enhancing your communication skills, developing your confidence level and trustworthy life, or living by the Six-L Principles, is possible.

Being attractive does not start with external beauty mostly, it comes from the within to the without. Approachable people often get attention because of their attitude and personal demeanour, not only because of their clothing, hairstyle or good looks. With good character, you can get positive attention from people regardless of your physical looks and social status.

In addition to all the discussions above and also to reiterate them, to build attractive and admirable personality, and draw people to yourself:

Walk with a Sense of Direction

When you have a vision or dream always in mind, you will show the world that you are positive with a direction. Your sense of direction tells people that you have purpose and you know where you are going, and this may prompt them to follow you. Your purpose with fortitude brings out the best in you and draw people's support.

Maintain consistency in your attitude, behaviour and direction. Consistency is a sign of character and character leads to respect and attention. Take calculated steps and do not compromise on your principles, vision and mission. Without consistency, people will not take you seriously. Some people will even manipulate you, if they know, you are not consistent. Believe in what you are doing, do it with all your heart and mind, and people will give you their support.

Pursue Your Dreams with Values

Pursue your purpose with a set of values and determination. Do what you can do best, and people will come requiring of your service. As stated earlier, John Wesley says that "when you set yourself on fire, people just love to come and see you burn." People have no business doing with idle hands.

In fact, the best friend of an idle hand is the devil. It is said that "the devil finds job for an idle hand." Occupy yourself with what will benefit you and others. Your popularity comes with your set values and principle. Be focused and pursue your purpose with all your strength, it enhances your self-image. Pursue your purpose with faithfulness, principle and strong conviction and you will attract and maintain relationships.

Maintain Positive Attitude through Challenges

In life there are adversities. Adversities are like hurdles to overcome. When you meet challenges have positive attitude. Focus on the positive side of your life and people who have difficulty seeing the brighter side of life, will be encouraged and they will come closer to you.

Never, never give up on life or your vision, because of problems you face. Odds may come your way, but with tenacity of purpose, you will overcome. Even, if you relate your problems to people, show them you are in control. Challenges may come, but your positive attitude during the challenging moments will draw people to you and maintain relationships.

Never abandon your principles and purpose because of troubles, if you do, you will lose your vision, your admirers and expel friends. Develop maximum spirit of endurance, firmness of purpose, and it will manifest itself in your external demeanour, and appearance.

Deal with Your Fears, Weaknesses and Personality Threats

Many at times we are constrained by our limitations; we think we are not worthy to approach some people or do certain things. But you need to look beyond your fears, deal with your challenges, gather courage and take positive steps. If you allow your fears or challenges to overcome you, these will become a blockade or an obstruction to your personal appeal. Your limitations will not limit you, if you do not limit yourself.

Deal with your weaknesses and do not allow anything or anybody to become a threat to your personal worth. Deal with your fears and weaknesses and manage your threats; see your threats as hurdles of opportunity. There are opportunities in every problem. Note that everybody has a weakness or the other, but how you manage it is important. Your ingenuity in managing your fears, threats or weaknesses makes you exceptional and outstanding.

Develop a Sense of Humour

Develop a sense of humour and smile easily. It is easier to approach people and feel happy with them, when they appear to be cheerful than, if they are moody. Negative attitudes turn people away from you, but comfortable attitude, as stated earlier, attracts people to you. Crack jokes a little and make people laugh out their problems once in a while. When conversing with people find sometime for fun moments, especially, when you are dealing with serious issues.

When people are in difficulties show them sympathy, but also try to give them some comic relief if possible, it will relieve them a little off their pains. People never forget their hilarious movements and people who make them happy. Some people have serious problems and they need comfortable people to be around them. Develop a sense of humour and you will draw many people to yourself. Cultivate genuine smiles that will not come off; it will be your valuable asset of personality.

Have Mentors and Role Models

There is a saying that "the person who cuts a path does not know whether the path is straight or crooked, it is those behind who can determine." To live a life which is worthy of emulation, you should get well experienced and virtuous people who will guide you. Personally, I have well experienced people in my country and abroad, who are mentors of my spiritual life, relationship, and purpose of life. Nobody is an epitome of knowledge, get mentors who can guide you to achieve your life dreams.

Also, find role models who have high ethical and moral standards and learn from their life. Let their life challenge you to improve upon yourself. Do not choose role models just because of their popularity; look at their purpose, values and what they stand for and compare it to your desired purpose and standards. Investigate their background and satisfy yourself first, before you draw inspiration from them or look up to them. Some of the personalities I use in the discussions are my role models on specific issues and life endeavours.

Life is guided by ideas, and these ideas become your principles which later, become your way of life and inform your lifestyle. Consequently, what you think of yourself that is what you are. If you think failure, failure will become your portion and you will be failure. Think positively of yourself and you will see your personality enhanced. Your attitude and people you relate to are very important. Positive minded people enhance your ability to be positive, but negative minded people take away the very little confidence you have. Avoid negative minds and identify with people with 'the can do spirit'; they help light up your path to possibilities.

Always remember that there are transforming stages of life, from birth to infancy, infancy to adolescence, adolescence to adulthood, and adulthood to old age. Each stage of life affects the other, in that sequential order. If you misconduct yourself at one stage of life, it will affect the other stages.

People misconduct themselves at their adolescence stage of life which had, and still have negative repercussions for their vision, job acquisition, social status and adult life. People misconduct themselves, whilst at school and their school records still affect their public lives today.

To live a life that you will not regret in future, identify the way of life and the kind of personality you desire. Perceive it in your mind, make a mental picture of it, and put it into action, until it is internalised to become part of your lifestyle. Train up yourself in the way you should go, so that when you grow up, you will not regret it.

A decision at a time affects the other; identify your desired personality, seek knowledge, make friend with wisdom, get guidance from level head people, and stay focus. James 3:17 says "The wisdom that is from above is first pure, then peaceable, gentle, willing to yield, full of mercy and *of* good fruits."

Once again, to be appreciated by society is not in your ability to please all people, accept all values, beliefs or civilisations, but your ability to identify your persona; who you are within the rules of the society and assume a progressive belief system, in consonance with the will of God; a belief system which motivates and inspires you. Have purpose, have principles, develop positive self-attitude, believe in your creator and identify with like-minded people who will have positive influence on you. Hold on to your principles, do good, love all, and have malice for none. You are an eagle, work on your personality and purpose, believe in yourself and you will draw many people to yourself to achieve your vision and mission.

Finally, truth adores a nation and its people, but dishonesty and deceit crumbles the very soul of a nation and its people. Build your confidence and let truth be your breastplate. Always remember that you are uniquely and wonderfully made in the image of God, with unique qualities which, if developed will enhance your personal life, and draw many people to you, who will support your course.

Beware of undermining yourself and your abilities; believe in yourself and always put your trust in God. May God strengthen and energise you to enhance your personality to fulfil your purpose, interest and passion for life.

BIBLIOGRAPHY 

Abernathy, Ralph (Rev), Newsweek Magazine 1-19-1998, "And the walls came tumbling down," Online Wikipedia, the free encyclopedia.mht.

Anderson, Jon Lee, Letter from Liberia, "After the Warlords," The New Yorker, 27 March 2006.

Andersen, Peter. (2007), "Nonverbal Communication: Forms and Functions" (2nd ed.), Waveland Press.

Bandura, Albert (1986) "Social foundations of thought and action" in, Ryckman M. Richard (1997), "Theories of Personality" (6th ed.), University of Maine at Corono, Brook/Cole Publishing Company.

Berens, V. Linda (2006), Understanding Yourself and Others: An Introduction to the 4 Temperaments-3.0, Telos Publications.

Bezdrob, Anne Marie du Preez (2006). "The Nelson Mandela Story," Samoja Books. ISBN 0-620-36570-6.

Britannica Online Encyclopaedia, "Ellen Johnson-Sirleaf" on Wikipedia, the free encyclopedia.mht.

Brydon, R. Steven& Scott D. Michael (200), "Between Oneand Many: The Art and Science of Public Speaking"

(3rd ed.) Mayfield Publication Company, ISBN 0-7674-0817-9.

Carver, C. S., & Scheier, M. F. (2000), "Perspectives on Personality" (4th ed.) Boston: Allyn and Bacon.

Churchill, Winston S. (1951), "The Second World War, Volume 5: Closing the Ring." Houghton Miffin Edition. Bantam Books, New York No ISBN. Online, Wikipedia, the free encyclopedia.mht.

Douglas, Martin "Esther Ocloo, 83, African Leader and Microlending Pioneer, Dies," obituary in New York Times, March 10, 2002, accessed on Africa Prize website.

Evans, Eric (2004). "Thatcher and Thatcherism." Routledge, ISBN 041527012X.

Eysenck, H. J. and Eysenck, S. G. B. (1965), "The Eysenck Personality Inventory."British Journal of Educational Studies, Vol. 14, No. 1.

Jung, C.J. (1921), "Psychologischen Typen."Rascher Verlag, Zurich - translated by H.G. Baynes, 1923.

Lincoln, Abraham (1858), "A House Divided Against Itself Cannot Stand," National Centre for Public Policy Research, www.nationalcenter.org

Lisa, Weseman, "4 Ways to Draw People to You, And it's not about looks. mht!

Lucas, E. Stephen (2001), "The Art of Public Speaking," (7th ed.), McGraw-Hill, International Edition ISBN 0-07-118003-6.

Ludwig, Emil (1956), "Abraham Lincoln and the Times that Tried His Soul" Liveright Publication Corporation, A Premier Book.

Luther King, Martin Jr. (1998), "Autobiography" Edited by Clayborne Carson.

Mair, George (1995). "Oprah Winfrey: The Real Story." Carol Publication Group, ISBN 1559722509.

Makeba Miriam (2009), Encyclopaedia Britannica Online, www.britannica.com

Maxwell, C. John, "Be a People Person," Joint Heir Publication, ISBN: 1-56476-264-5.

Mehrabian and Ferris (1967), "Inference of Attitude from Nonverbal Communication in Two Channels" in, The Journal of Counselling Psychology, Vol.31.

Milton, Joyce (1999) "The First Partner: Hillary Rodham Clinton." William Morris. ISBN 0-688-15501-4, Online Wikipedia, the free encyclopedia.mht.

New King James Version Bible (NKJV) and Revise Standard Version, on www.powerbible.com

Nicolson, Harold (1967), "The War Years 1939-1945, Diaries and Letters," vol. II, New York: Athenaeum. Wikipedia, the free encyclopedia.mht.

Nkrumah, Kwame (1957), "Ghana: The Autobiography of Kwame Nkrumah" ISBN 0-901787-60-4.

Peale, V. Norman, "The Power of Positive Thinking," Rhyma Research Institute Inc. 449-01450-095.

Poe, D. Zizwe (2003), "Kwame Nkrumah's Contribution to Pan-African Agency," New York: Routledge.

Rick,Gettle (2004), "Developing Your Personality, Presence, Magnetism, And Relationship Skills," online, www.successercising.com

Ron Kurtus (20 March, 2007), "Three Character Trait Classifications," online, www.school-for-champions.com

Russell, M. (May, 2006), "Personal Appearance and Attitude," online www. ezinearticles.com

Schultz, D., & Schultz, S.E. (1994), "Theories of Personality" (5th ed.) Pacific Grove, CA: Brooks/Cole/Columnists/BenShapiro/2003/03/19/.

Shapiro, Ben (March 19, 2003)."The Oprah schnook club," online, wwww.townhall.com

Quotations from Bible Power CD, www.powerbible.com

Spink, Kathryn (1997). "Mother Teresa: A Complete Authorized Biography." New York. HarperCollins, ISBN 0-06-250825-3, Online Wikipedia, the free encyclopedia.mht.

Tim LaHaye, (1984), "Why You Act the Way You Do" Tyndale House Publishers ISBN 0842382127.

Tim LaHaye, (1984), "Your Temperament: Discover Its Potential" Tyndale House Publishing, ISBN 0842362207.

Tom Marshall (1991), "Understanding Leadership," Sovereign World International Book, ISBN 1 85240 053 6.

This book deals with how you can strategically develop your career. It helps you discover, make career choices, set your career goals, plan and develop your career. It helps you set achievable career goals with the right information and work on your goals to achieve success in your career.

ComBEL Publications
Tel:233 243 538 726
Email:combelgh@gmail.com
www.combelgh.com*

ISBN: 978-9988-1-2605-6

9 789988 126056